Codependency

Table of Contents

Introduction

What is codependency? Where did the term come from? We'll explore the history of codependency and give a thorough definition, so you can understand what we're talking about throughout the book. We'll also briefly explain the different types of relationships where codependency is present, how a codependent might behave in their relationship, and where codependency comes from. Why talk about the history first? Codependency is a term with a very specific origin story, and knowing how it's changed over the years will help guide us through the rest of the book.

The Evolution Of "Codependency"

The term "codependency" can be traced back to the treatment of alcoholism. In 1936, Alcoholics Anonymous became the first organization to treat alcoholism as an illness and not a personal failing. The concept of the 12-Step Program caught on. Years later, in 1951, a 12-step recovery program for the *families* and *partners* of alcoholics was created. By the 1970's, treatment centers started to see the importance of including family, partners, and social communities in the process. They used the term "co-alcoholic" to describe the alcoholic's significant other.

Following alcohol treatment's path, people started seeing the similarities with drug addictions and adopted their strategies for recovery. Programs started using the term "chemical dependency" to describe all chemical and drug addictions. To match, co-alcoholism became "co-chemically dependent," and then "co-dependent."

That background is important, because on the surface, codependent might sound like it's describing a relationship where both members are dependent *on each other*. However, the term actually means that the person in a relationship with someone who has a dependency on alcohol or drugs is, by proxy, also dependent. In the 1980's, with the creation of this new term and programs, treatment started to include codependents more and develop help specifically for them.

Now, the codependency term has expanded beyond chemical dependency. Instead of alcohol or drugs, the elephant in the room could be a mental illness, abuse, or even a negative trait like selfishness or irresponsibility. Though the types of relationships where codependency can be found vary, symptoms are strikingly similar:

- The codependent lives in denial
- The codependent always wants to please and take care of others
- The codependent obsesses over the person(s) they are codependent on
- The codependent struggles with low self-esteem, depression, and other challenging emotions

Types Of Codependency

There are four types of relationships where codependency is a common result: one with addiction, one that's abusive, one with mental illness, and one where one of the members is very insecure. A relationship where addiction is present is the classic formula for codependency. For the addict, their addiction (whether it's alcohol or drugs) will always come first, and change is very difficult, especially without treatment. The addict's partner is the one who is codependent, and surrenders control over to the addict. Everything is about accommodating the addiction and making excuses for the addict.

In abusive relationships, the target of the abuse is the codependent one. They give up their power to their abusive partner. The abuse can be emotional, physical, or both. While a relationship may not have initially been abusive, it can become that way. The targeted partner develops codependent tendencies out of fear or a hope that the abuse will stop.

The third type of relationship is one that involves mental illness. The codependent is not the one who is struggling with the mental health issue, but they surrender power to the illness and negative symptoms like antisocial behavior. The codependency is most evident when the mentally-ill partner is not seeking treatment. We want to emphasize there are lots of relationships where someone is mentally ill and codependency is not present. Codependency appears when the mentally-ill party is not seeking or receiving treatment. Some untreated mental illnesses or disorders can result in abuse, like narcissistic personality disorder.

The last type of relationship where codependency can arise doesn't involve addiction, abuse, or mental illness. The person who is codependent is simply very afraid of being alone, usually because of past trauma or bad relationships. The codependent puts up with their partner's selfishness, immaturity, or other bad behaviors because they don't want to do anything to make their partner leave them.

Passive vs. active

Within codependent relationships, the codependent can either be active or passive. Passive codependents avoid conflict and tend to live in fear of being abandoned. Passive codependents are frequently found in abusive relationships or relationships with narcissists. Rather than confront their partner about issues, they develop more subtle strategies, which can make them appear to be the manipulative one.

Active codependents are not afraid to speak their minds, but they are still afraid to make big changes like actually breaking up with their partner. They will complain about how they are treated and might engage in lots of arguments, but they feel powerless to change their situation. They live in the hope that their partner will change and things will get better.

What Is Codependency?

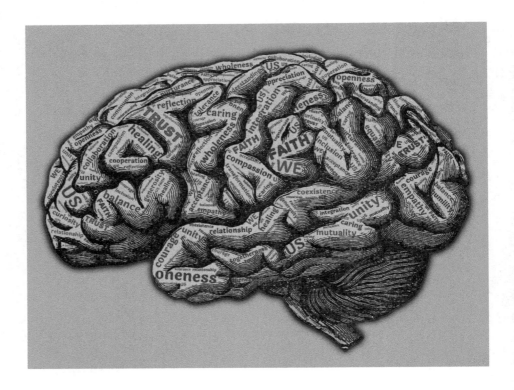

The term "codependency" is quite misleading and inaccurate. A more dependent clause would be "external dependency." The term codependence erupted into the consciousness of people in the last few years because of the vital truth contained in its message.

It is of great importance to note that the definition of codependence has drastically changed with time. It is a term that has dynamically expanded since the time it was birthed.

Briefly, I would be explaining the evolution of codependency to clear up some misunderstandings. An example of disagreement is the dictionary meaning of the term.

There are many other definitions of codependency. However, from all of them, it was shown that the term codependency is commonly identified with Alcoholics Anonymous (AA) groups. The origin of codependency can be traced to how the non-alcoholic members of a family were affected by another's alcoholism.

Some attempts were made to conceptualize the term with the framework of a disease model.

First, it was proposed that codependency was a maladaptive behavior and illness which was developed as a result of being in close contact with someone with chronic impalement. Then, it was proposed that it was an addiction disorder that resulted from a person's failed attempt to control inner feelings by controlling other people and other events outside one's self. Third, it was characterized as interdependent and an attachment of people to alcohol, drugs, and medication, sex, work, and money.

Another attempt was made to conceptualize the term with the framework of personality disorder. This brought about the definition that codependency is a form of personality that encompasses several traits; neglecting individual needs, feeling of constriction, control tendencies, denial, depression, and stress-related psychological illnesses.

Codependency was also conceptualized within the perspective of social interaction. It was characterized as an exogenous and endogenous phenomenon, which is inter-personal and intra-personal.

With all these, codependency is said to be a complex construct which is characterized by a wide range of psychological, yet negative terms. The popularization of the word "codependency" has had both positive and negative consequences for family therapy. On the positive side, it has helped raise public awareness of the kind of relationship that takes place in alcoholic families. It has provided a sort of appreciation for the role that is assumed by everyone in the family, where alcoholism, which is viewed as a severe psychological disorder, occurs. In such families, children may take on specific responsibilities such as ensuring the doors are locked because their alcoholic parents are too drunk to do so, or have passed out. In this situation, the children begin to act as parents at a delicate age. No one in the family would be immune from the effect alcoholism has brought into the family, and everyone would have to contribute to the maintenance of the problem.

A codependent person is somewhat addicted to a wrong pattern of relating to other people. It is sometimes learned from an abusive home or from following some specific oppressive rules in a home. All these would lead to loss of authenticity, intimacy denial, spiritual sterility, and we remain strangers to ourselves. All these would be explained more as we move along. Codependency is more of learned behavior. There are three "temperament dimensions" which are defined according to an individual's response to novelty, danger or punishment, and reward. These three factors are called novelty seeking, harm avoidance, and reward dependence. A person prone to seeking novelty is always at risk and in crisis. These situations can cause the brain to release a chemical known as dopamine, which influences cognition, motivation, and motor control. In a family, novelty seekers are the scapegoats. They take risks outside the family and then use it along with uncertainty and crisis within the family to cause the production of the chemical, dopamine.

For the reward dependent individuals, they define their self-worth based on position, accomplishment, power, and possession. They can sometimes be aggressive and trying to control people around him through covert or overt methods. Now instead of producing dopamine, norepinephrine would be released. It is connected with memory, concentration, and also fight-or-flight response. This particular person always wants to be the hero of the family or the person in charge. An example of a reward dependent person is a workaholic. This person is always striving to get a raise or get a better job or expecting a breakthrough.

The harm avoidance person does their best to maintain the status quo they have tried to portray in the minds of people. They tend to play it safe to avoid ricks, and this allows for the production of serotonin, also regarded as a natural tranquilizer. It also enables dysfunction through their inaction.

If codependency remains untreated, it is likely to stretch an individual beyond his or her limit. When it has gotten to this point, the body will release epinephrine, cortisol, and norepinephrine, which primes the body for reaction and action.

Cognitive confusion shows up on two different levels in codependents. In the first, the individual, though aware of what they think, will not share it until they know that thought will be accepted. At the second level, the codependent does not know what they believe, and their mind will go blank, or ideas will become jumbled when asked. It stretches from simple opinions such as a favorite color to an inability to recognize and label emotions the codependent is feeling.

Some dysfunctional pattern in a family includes;

a. A physically abusive family system
b. A sexually abusive family system
c. A psychologically disturbed family system
d. An emotionally disturbed family system
e. A rigidly religious family system.

Codependent beings are so entangled with another human being that they become addicts. Their identity becomes crowded out by the other person's problems.

When a person is codependent on another, he or she does for others what they can do for themselves. They suffer from fear of abandonment.

The existential emptiness is mostly concerned with the way you relate to living, while the other, which is the psychological emptiness is concerned with how you connect with yourself. It is correlated by depression and also quite related to shame. Depression does not come to you all at once. It first sends its babies to you to prepare the way for it. These babies are the symptoms of depression, guilt, poor concentration, sleeping habits, restlessness or anxiety, sadness, change in or loss of appetite, negative thoughts often suicidal and the feeling of emptiness. It is now up to you to either open up yourself for the arrival of these babies or you work something out.

There are specific causes of psychological emptiness. For codependents who are addicted to unhealthy things, their type of emptiness comes from their childhood. Their families were deprived of sufficient nurturing and empathy, which is referred to as **abandonment depression**. Codependents experience this on different levels. They experience the ill effects of self-distance, disengagement, and disgrace, which can be veiled by the behaviors that go with habit, including denial, reliance, people-pleasing, control, caretaking, obsession, impulsive conduct, and emotions, for example, outrage and anxiety.

Sometimes chronic failure to get sufficient sympathy and satisfaction of requirements in childhood can significantly influence our feeling of self and having a place in adulthood. Physical division or emotional abandonment as from childhood from parents affects how, as grown-ups we experience being distant from everyone else, the cutting off of a relationship, demise, or other colossal misfortune. Pity, depression or void, can initiate sentiments of disgrace and the other way around. Regularly, these early deficiencies are exacerbated by trauma, violence and abuse, and relinquishment later in immaturity and adult relationships. A codependent person would often seem rigid, more like a perfectionist. They would find anything that works best for them within their limited world view and then force themselves to operate within that frame of mind. There are consequences for this kind of behavior, but the major one is that they would have a sort of judgmental attitude towards others. The primary deficiency of codependent individuals is that they must judge anyone outside their frame of mind or framework. This kind of rigidity often plays out in risk refusal. Their mode of thinking is if no one is pleased, it is a risk. Everyone must be happy but themselves. They see love as risky, change as unsafe, care for themselves as hazardous too. It is quite unfortunate that all these are necessary to overcome codependency.

Life is not an emergency! This is a big deal! Codependents reliably lived in a high-stress vortex—startled of individuals, deserting, and life itself.

They stress such a significant amount over everything that was outside of their control—regularly, other individuals. They ought to understand that life is intended to be delighted in and enjoyed. Great and terrible things will occur, however with a focused and well-balanced heart, they can get over any hindrances.

The way to adjust and be well-balanced is to live entirely in each minute, tolerating life for what it is. In any event, when you are feeling down, you should realize that the Universe has your back, and everything in life is unfurling as it should.

On the off chance that you don't hold this conviction, it may recall that you have your own back, and you can deal with whatever is coming. At the point when you trust in yourself, and spotlight on yourself rather than others, it's a lot simpler to appreciate life and quit living in dread.

Codependent relationships are marked by attempts to control the acts of others. These relationships are always disrespectful because people will be prevented from developing responsibility, the other person would be seen as the center of life, and both individuals would be robbed of making personal decisions.

Codependency often rises as a result of family dysfunction, and the codependents struggle with an unhealthy understanding of the word loyalty. As loyalty is typically understood as a virtue, it has also become a liability if abused. These dysfunctional families would create lies that would emphasize the importance of family or say that family issues are to be discussed inside the family and not outside. Then, the codependent would be unable and unwilling to betray the family's trust by keeping quiet and not seeking help from anyone outside the family. This level of secrecy can allow people to pull back from relationships basically for fear of revealing family secrets to outsiders.

Codependents may display a variety of behavioral tendencies. An attempt at self-sufficiency runs behind many of these behavioral patterns. While many codependents struggle with low self-esteem, others choose to forge forward on their own, refusing help. In this way, codependents betray an unhealthy fear of the world because only the individual herself can be trusted. It helps protect the codependent partner, leaving little or no opportunity for people to hurt him or her.

Murphy and Leonard provide examples of codependency are a broad sense of the term. Though there is no physical substance in Murphy's life, he is still exceedingly independent of the approval of others. He is addicted to meeting the expectations of others that he, has significant difficulty taking care of his own needs and desires, or even commenting with his independent thoughts and feelings, this loss of self-awareness and failure to attend to his personal needs as he seems to please others have reflected majorly on his psychological dependency.

Leonard, on the other hand, fears to upset his wife and her parents by turning them down. It is a sign of codependency. He wants to be the good son-in-law, does not want to be responsible for the anger and disappointment of his wife and in-laws, and because of this, he decided to stay quiet. At any price, he would keep his peace. Trust me; if he were not codependent, he would have been able to tell him, in-laws and wife, to take responsibility for their decisions and role in heaving a good family relationship instead of shouldering him with a feeling of responsibility for their insensitivity to his feelings.

Some people, mostly women, were taught to be dependent. They learned how to live their lives and to be cared for by people. Many people fear to be alone, and that is a part of being human. According to research, nothing would destroy emotional security faster than loving someone who is dysfunctional. People living with these problems demand others to center their lives on and on them. Trust me; the healthiest of us humans may still doubt ourselves after living with dysfunctional. When this happens, they become victims of us and love evaporates and then, we begin to lose the ability to take care of ourselves.

Specific ideas could help gain grounds;

- Learn to finish businesses as often and as best as you can. Figure out how such businesses of the past are affecting your present and future. Get some perspective.

- Cherish the needy, vulnerable child inside you and nurture them. A child is a person who can never totally disappear. What is the fun in that? You would be as stuck up as a nail. So, no matter how self-sufficient you become, the child will not disappear. That child would cry out when you become stressed. The child demands attention when in need and when it is least expected.

- Do not look unto others to gain happiness. It is said that the source of joy is inside us and not from others. So, you must learn to center yourself in yourself, not in other-selves.

- Depend on yourself as it is expected of you. Not everyone would be there for you when you want them to, so you can start being there for yourself.

- Strive for independence or interdependence. Try by first examining the ways to be dependent both financially and emotionally on people around you.

Are You Codependent?

Throughout our lives as we grow as individuals, we will develop new relationships and at the same time, break off old ones that we do not deem fit any longer. Our day-to-day life is not only composed of ourselves but of others too. We will involve ourselves in healthy relationships that have a foundation of trust, love, respect, and compassion, and others which may be unhealthy and involve volatility, distrust, poor communication, and lack of support.

One of these unhealthy relationship dynamics is known as codependency. Codependency affects an individual emotionally and behaviorally, where they are unable to have a balanced and healthy relationship where both parties are mutually supporting and tending to the needs of the other. Another term that is commonly used in place of codependency is "relationship addiction" as the individual is seen as dependent on the relationship and feel overly responsible for the other's behavior. Although the codependent person has good intentions and aims to care for their partner, parent, sibling or friend who has an addiction or is ill, the desire to help becomes obsessive and the individual ends up feeling helpless and on the road to destruction.

How To Identify Codependency

An easy way to identify codependent behaviors is through self-worth and self-esteem. Those who are codependent seek gratification and happiness through external sources and generally have low self-esteem. They often feel a compulsion to 'save' or 'rescue' the other party in the hopes of receiving feelings of satisfaction from the sheer fact of 'being needed'. Some common characteristics of codependent people include:

Inability to set healthy boundaries

A healthy relationship has set boundaries which are limits to understanding what is 'ours' and what is 'theirs' in terms of emotions, problems, and even our identity. Those who are codependent often take on others' emotions, problems, and even parts of their identity, and this is why a codependent's lack of self-identity tends to occur.

With healthy boundaries, we know what our rights are and we know that we deserve respect. We know when to say 'no' and we know when others have ulterior motives and are simply taking advantage of us. Codependents gradually develop an overwhelming tolerance for suffering and distress and can't enforce appropriate limits.

Trouble identifying feelings

Because of the abundance of painful emotions that surface from being codependent, the individual feels trapped and is unable to identify why they feel anxiety, rejection, feelings of failure that eventually develop into hopelessness and resentment. Apathy is also common in codependents, as all these feelings can become overwhelming and merge together. This makes it difficult to effectively identify each emotion and find ways of dealing with them.

Poor communication

Communication is what strengthens the barrier between the codependent and the other party. The codependent individual finds it challenging to communicate their feelings, thoughts, and needs but because they have trouble identifying their feelings, it makes it even more difficult to do so. Codependent individuals are also fearful of not being seen as useful or valuable; therefore, being truthful isn't one of their strong points. They are afraid that what they say will be misperceived and distort the truth in order to protect themselves.

Excessive need to avoid feelings of abandonment

Codependents thrive on being needed. This means that any sign of rejection or abandonment is seen as a threat and they will do anything to ensure that they play a part in helping the relationship succeed and thrive. The codependent relies on affection and the constant of receiving confirmation from their loved one.

Need for approval/to please others

Approval seeking can become an addictive behavior for codependents. Just like someone addicted to drugs, the individual constantly needs approval in order to feel in control. The concept of validation can become powerful and this can quickly become the default mechanism by which the codependent deals with their insecurities and their current emotional state.

Controlling behavior

The codependent has an obsession with control due to the blurred boundaries discussed previously. Everyone around them and their actions are a reflection of themselves, so they feel as though they need to control their behavior so others will comply. They have a certain expectation for others to meet their standards, and advice is in fact, instruction.

Intense sense of responsibility for the behavior of others

Empathy and sympathy are natural emotions to feel when people who are close to you endure difficult times. Codependents take this to the next level and feel as though they are responsible for the other party's feelings and problems.

Obsessions/fear/anxiety

For codependents, anxiety is a natural occurrence. Relationships are seen as unpredictable and fragile, so individuals anticipate and worry about the worst. Emotional mistreatment from the past can manifest in the present as fear of criticism, failure, vulnerability, and not being in control.

Low self-esteem

Numerous studies prove that good self-esteem and relationship satisfaction have a direct correlation. Codependents tend to have low self-esteem and develop an unhealthy attachment style. These have a detrimental effect on true intimacy and actions that seem to foster closeness actually drive the other party away.

Unhealthy perception of love

A healthy love often refers to an interdependent relationship where both parties have a close personal relationship with each other that provides them with what they need to feel cared for and comfortable in the relationship. Codependency is one-sided - it is not often mutually-satisfying as the codependent lives their lives based on and through their significant other.

Difficulty making decisions

Codependents typically have trouble making decisions for themselves. Their decision-making abilities seem to be all used up to help others make decisions. Being neglected in their childhood can often cause a lack of assertiveness where the individual denies their needs and feelings, so they don't risk a reaction from the other party.

Are You In A Codependent Relationship?

If you are trying to find time to be with your partner, then there is a big tendency that you might be trying too hard to be always there for your loved one. But what is wrong with waking up, brushing your teeth, eating every meal, and going to work and back home with your partner? Even if all the Disney films and love songs are trying to say that it is part of love to always want to be with a lover, it would apparently cause you a lot of problems in the long run.

Defining A Codependent Relationship

A codependent relationship can be shaped into the most romantic relationship that you can think of where it is almost impossible for you to live without each other. You may find yourself wanting to be in the same space with the man or woman of your dreams, and be with your loved one every single moment of the day.

If you tend to think that your world revolves around your partner, and you might as well die if you separate ways, then it creates a big void in your life when you face problems, or even separation. Many people find themselves being unable to recover after a divorce or breakup when they get too used to having their loved one around.

Here are the telltale signs that you are in a codependent relationship:

1. You think that your relationship is more important than anything else

You are willing to leave your career, your family, and friends just to be with your partner. If religion forbids your relationship, then the most appealing solution is to change your faith, and nothing else. Think of it as Romeo and Juliet type of relationship – when you are going against the odds, you might as well die together because well, love is all that matters.

2. You have been a little too unselfish in your relationship.

You tend to give it all to your partner, even if it is your credit card or the last dollar in your wallet, he/she can have it. It does not matter if you would be unable to visit your parents this weekend, as long as you can be the date for the movie that your partner is dying to watch. It also would not matter if you have to work on a double shift, as long as your partner would not have to worry about paying this month's rent.

3. You put in more effort than your partner.

You would mind if your partner tells you that you have to go to the grocery alone because it is baseball night with the boys. You would also find yourself in a lot of situations wherein you put in most of your money for conjugal expenses such as house and car loans, or for your wedding. You don't mind it much that your partner does not do any of the chores at home.

4. You are disconnected from other people.

Your friends may seem to be quite distant from you because you don't show up at any of the gatherings that you are invited to. If you ever show, all that you can talk about is your relationship, or you show up with your partner. Your Facebook is entirely made up of pictures featuring you and your man, and how happy you are together. That is probably the only time that your friends and family do get to hear from you.

5. You tend to always like what your partner likes.

You never really liked Mexican food, and a year ago, you hate it. But it is the only type of food your partner eats, and if he likes it, maybe you should too. You also love to buy everything for two, and you have a couple shirt (in his favorite brand, of course) for every occasion.

You also begin loving baseball and beer, and you begin having interests in absurd positions your partner begs to do in bed. You know that you do not like lovemaking that way, but if your partner likes it, then it must be good.

6. You feel responsible for how your partner behaves.

You always see the good in your partner, and if it seems that people are offended by the way he acts in public, you serve as his PR/apologist. When your partner gets in a brawl or suddenly leaves the party, you make sure that everyone knows that he is a good person deep down inside. You see to it that everyone knows that he is just having a bad day, and that he really is a sweet guy.

7. You strongly want attention and approval.

You begin making groaning sounds whenever you see your boyfriend texts someone at work, or when he is watching TV. That is your signal that you should cuddle. You also love making letters or sweet nothings more frequently now. You begin shopping for clothes that make you feel attractive. You like to shop with your boyfriend so that he can tell you the clothes that you should wear. You like yourself better when he tells you that you are beautiful. You don't feel beautiful when he is not around.

8. You hate being left alone.

You begin being jealous of his friends, and you do not want to sit alone in your couch and wait until he returns. On another note, you also would rather be alone than hang out with your friends. You feel that you are becoming afraid of his attention wandering elsewhere, and you wish that he'd always take you.

9. You ignore red flags, even the most obvious ones.

There are countless times that he lied to you, but it does not matter as long as he stays. You forgive him easily when he has some flings over the years, and it is okay that he slapped you or dragged you home when he was upset. He already said sorry, and you are sure that he meant it. Even if he said sorry for the same mistake for the nth time, you know that he still meant it.

Codependency Is A Problem

You may not realize it, but if one or both of you, exhibit these characteristics, you may soon find yourself in a painful situation. Even if you think that this is the right way to run a relationship, you may be gravely mistaken.

Codependency is considered a problem because it is an addiction, and it prevents you to exhibit actions that would be more helpful and nurturing to a relationship. One of those actions that are really important is becoming yourself. It is an addiction because it makes you behave in such a way that you restrict yourself by being obsessed on labels that could possibly not fit your relationship anyway. In the end, you may find yourself wanting your partner to behave in ways that you desire.

Isn't That Normal?

People would always have sets of expectations in a relationship, and that is normal. However, making you and your partner live according to those expectations may be too extreme. After all, you and your partner would soon change, and you may find out things about each other that you may not have expected.

Relationships that function well make allowances, but codependency does not. In a sense, it is that certain desire that makes you want your partner to always behave like a prince charming, or that certain obsession to make a bad boy material turn into a perfect gentleman, just the way you see in the movies.

However, you know that it may not happen, and it may seriously hurt your loved one to see you disappointed. You may also find yourself changing to fit instead into a certain type of person that is designed to fit your lover. In the end, you may not also do your relationship a favor when you do so. Believe it or not, a lot of relationships fail because of these seemingly-normal things to do while people are still dating or already married. It appears that not a lot of people understand that there are certain allowances they should make in a relationship. One can blame it on the movies, but codependency can be seen as a serious attitude problem.

However, we live in a society that seriously tolerates it. There is the pressure of family standards, and we often try to figure out who among the people we date is the spouse-material, or not. We exist in a world full of labels, and in the end, we get frustrated when our expectations are not met. However, codependents go to the extreme, in the belief that anyone can turn out to be that very desirable person if they force compromise into the relationship. Sometimes though, compromises can become a little bit too extreme.

How to Avoid Codependent Relationships

Prevention is better than cure. This is true not just in medicine, but also in relationships. As you enter a new relationship, it feels as if everything falls into place. You could not foresee any difficulties or tendencies that it might become an abusive, codependent relationship. However, there will be times when tensions and issues arise. Codependency could not be avoided unless you acknowledge the symptoms and always be *aware of yourself*.

Self-awareness is key if you would like to avoid codependency in your future or present relationship. It is important to take a step back, take a breath, and reconsider what is happening to your relationship.

How To Avoid Becoming Codependent

Look at yourself. Evaluate. Do you have addictive tendencies? Have you had experiences of substance abuse, or are you currently abusing one?

Before you enter a relationship, make sure that you are in your *best form* and is emotionally and mentally ready for a relationship.

Always remember that relationships are not like the movies or novels where it is all about the feeling. Relationships in real life take work, effort, and partnership in order to succeed.

This is always a product of mutual investment by two people. If you do not know what real love is, or is currently having personal problems in your life, how can you successfully be in a relationship?

The best way to avoid a codependent relationship is to make sure that you are a healthy, self-sufficient individual before you enter one.

Be in a relationship not because you *need* it; be there because it is for the betterment of your character and individuality.

You should remember that codependency starts from needs that turn into addiction.

Always ask yourself: *What does this relationship mean to me? What am I getting out of it?*

Always be aware if you are "giving too much" or "needing" too much from the relationship. Feelings of love and acceptance are very beautiful, satisfactory feelings, but anything in excess is harmful.

This can always lead to addiction. These feelings can even serve as a blindfold when your relationship starts to take the abusive turn.

How To Evaluate Your Relationships

Satisfying relationships can only be described by one word: *satisfactory*. A good relationship should be good enough for you to stay in and invest your feelings in consciously. It should complement you as a person and make you feel whole.

There is no such thing as a "perfect" relationship. There will always be differences and disagreements between two persons. You two may feel as if you have a perfect union or chemistry, but relationships are a completely different matter. There will always be compromise and imperfections in a relationship. You would need to establish *healthy bounds* between the two of you in order to avoid codependency, which will ruin the relationship and make it abusive.

Are you over-praising your relationship? A sign that you are starting to become codependent is when you describe everything as overly perfect even when there are cracks and gaps in the relationship.

A healthy relationship is one that has bounds set (such as privacy and so on) as well as a shared aspect between two people.

Each of you needs to grow as individuals of your own. If you feel as if your world is revolving around the relationship, then you should take a step back and reevaluate.

Be honest to yourself: Do you have a life outside the relationship? If this relationship didn't exist in your life, where would you be now?

If you can't answer this question, this means that you have become codependent or are starting to become codependent. You need to set bounds as early as possible to avoid further addiction to the relationship.

How To Set Bounds And Keep Everything Normal

If your relationship is fairly new, it is normal to wish that you could be with this person in every single day and in every single moment.

This is the honeymoon phase of the relationship.

However, as time passes, you should learn to set boundaries that, when crossed, signals that one person or the other is becoming *too demanding* or *abusive* in the relationship.

It is important to talk about what the two of you want or don't want in the relationship. Be vocal about this.

It might seem as if this is unnecessary since you are "perfectly in sync" and in love with each other, but you should understand that this is the best way to avoid abuse and codependency in the relationship. Learn to talk as two mature persons who respect one another.

What would you consider hurtful? When does giving and asking for attention become stressful for the two of you? Discuss these matters and respect the compromise and the solution that you would come up. No matter what happens, always put respect each other.

More importantly, *have self-respect.* Codependency and abuse in relationships usually occur because people let abuse happen to them.

How To Address The Potential Break-Out Of Codependency

Does your partner keep on crossing the boundaries that you two have set? Do they always commit mistakes and end up apologizing to you?

On the other side, does your partner tolerate your ill-character and does not feel upset when you cross the boundaries of the relationship? Does your partner allow you to lose self-respect and sacrifice your own happiness and well-being, yet still encourage you to be in the relationship?

It is difficult to accept the fact that things can turn wrong in a relationship. Sometimes, a relationship is just not designed to work.

If mistakes have been repeatedly occurring and you keep making amends, but nothing turns out right in the end, you should address the situation before you become addicted to the cycle.

If you are feeling miserable but tell yourself that you *still love* being in the relationship, you are at risk of becoming codependent.

Talk to your partner and threaten to leave if the situation does not improve.

This may be very difficult for you, but you can always reclaim yourself after the break up.

If you do not see each other maturing as individuals, and if the relationship seems like a prison that hinders the growth of the two of you, then the best option is to *leave* or *take a break* before one of you starts to become codependent.

Do not fall in love with abusive relationships. It will never turn out right in the end. Your happiness and your well-being is your responsibility.

Ending a Codependent Relationship

If you draw several rings and place a person in the center, every ring that expands from the center to the outer edges is people that have influenced them. The ring that is closest to the middle is the people who have the strongest influence on them like their partner or children. This will make them care about how their family feels, the way their family behaves, and what their family thinks. Someone who is codependent relies extremely heavily on the way their partner influences them. They don't just care about what their family feels, thinks, or does. They need their family to define who they are. Their partner turns into their ego mirror. They become a person with whom they can count on the show them their value and self-esteem. The bad news is this mirror doesn't have grey areas; it will reflect in either completely black or white. This means they see themselves as either damaged or perfect.

Ego Mirror

This term gets used to describe either one person or several people who get used by a codependent person to substitute the way they look at themselves. People who have well-formed, intact identities don't have a need for an ego mirror. They know themselves inside out. They don't identify with how they are reflected for somebody else. They listen to people whose opinion they value and when they care for. Anybody else won't be able to rock their foundation by disagreeing with them, judging them, or having conflicting needs.

If you think back to your childhood, you probably remember the story of "Snow White," the evil queen continuously goes to her mirror and asks if she is still "fairest of them all." The codependent person's partner is that mirror. Just like this evil queen, a codependent person has to be constantly reassured that they are superior. They can't even handle being told the truth. They need their mirror to tell them that they are the best. If they are ever told they aren't the best, they will fly into a rage and will try to destroy whatever caused their misery. They will basically "smash" their mirror.

A codependent person's identity could be shattered easily because it is so brittle. This is why they are desperate to change all negative feelings no matter the cost. They don't know how to change themselves inwardly, so they have to change on the outside. If push comes to shove, and if it means breaking the mirror, they won't hesitate to break it. Until it gets to that point, they will use any weapon they have at their disposal to force people to get rid of all concerns that might show that they aren't perfect.

Codependent people don't have the freedom to let other people be who they truly are. They can't stand to see others angry with them. They can't stand for anybody to think badly of them or be disappointed with them. They are tied to a certain reflection forever. They are in a place of pain since the only way for them to feel good about themselves is to make sure the mirror reflects them well.

Let's see how you answer these questions:

- Do you get panicky if you think your partner is mad at you and you don't know why?

- Are you constantly desperate that your partner knows your point?

- Do you give in to your partner's needs and then feel resentful?

- Can you handle it if your partner gets mad at you? Do you ever try to change how they feel?

- Do you feel uncomfortable if your partner asks for your opinion without telling you theirs?

- If you are having a deep discussion do you try to figure out how your partner feels before you ever share your feelings?

- Do you ever take your partner's advice and think it over without getting defensive?

- If you have expressed opinions that aren't the same, is there a way you can agree to disagree with them?

- Are you always aware of your partner's moods?

- Do you begin to get anxious if your partner walks away or ends a discussion before the conflict is resolved?

- If your partner criticizes you, is there a way you can listen without explaining yourself in different ways?

If you said yes to at least one of these questions, get out your journal and write about it. Think about a time that you reacted this way to your partner. Figure out if you can find a way to talk them out of how they feel, why you have to have their approval or are always trying to convince them of your position. If you need your partner approve of each action, though, and feeling, you may be using them as your ego mirror.

Ego Mirrors, Guilt, And Codependency

A person who is a narcissist and a person who is codependent will be lacking the same things at their core. Neither one has a healthy identity of themselves. Beneath the narcissist's bravado is a person who needs everybody else to validate their ego. Their ego mirror needs to show that "the world revolves around me," "better than thou," and a puffed-up sense of themselves. If they see any faults, inadequacies, or imperfections, the mirror is horribly wrong.

Narcissists won't feel guilty because they don't have any conflicts with their identity. They are perfectly okay with the idealized self. They just need their ego mirror to make sure they are shining pure white all the time. If the mirror doesn't give this to them, they try to find a new one. A narcissist's reflection looks like a perfect diamond to them at all times but unfortunately, it is just a big piece of glass.

For a person who is codependent, their identity always looks like a gem with flaws. It has blemishes, cracks, and its color will be off just a little bit. This isn't saying that they are undesirable, they just aren't perfect. Each diamond is just as shiny as all the other diamonds, but a codependent person knows there are flaws. They have conflicts since they know the flaws are always there. They just can't accept their flaws. They need that ego mirror to show them their brilliance instead of their flaws.

A person who has positive self-esteem and healthy ego will accept their imperfections along with other people's imperfections. A person who is codependent can't. They won't ever accept their flaws and work extremely hard to deny them. They have to see themselves as shiny and possessing wonderful qualities at all times. They try to be selfless, helpful, considerate, loving, and thoughtful. If they ever realize that they aren't, they start feeling guilty. If they happen to see their flaws in their ego mirror, they will never be able to accept it, even though they know it is true. Instead of looking deep inside themselves, they just attack the mirror.

Misdirected Guilt

You know that codependent people have an unrealistic sense of self. Their behavior may not match up to their distorted self-image. If this were to happen, they always blame the ego mirror.

Wes and Shirley have been with each other for over 22 years. Shirley is turning 50 and has been diagnosed with multiple sclerosis. Shirley's doctor meets with them and talks about the changes they can expect to happen with this disease. He takes a lot of time with them trying to help them learn how this illness is going to change their lives.

Shirley has always worked hard and is now going to have to limit her activities in order to keep her healthy. The doctor has asked Wes to make sure Shirley doesn't overdo it. He asks them to sit down and adjust their chores to help with Shirley's illness. Wes assures the doctor that he totally supports and understands Shirley. He is more than willing and happy to take on extra chores.

It takes them about a week to finally sit down and talk about what they are going to do. Wes agrees to do all the chores while Shirley will do more sedentary work like dealing with phone calls, paying the bills, and cooking. If any of their friends ask how Shirley is doing, Wes always makes a point of telling them that he is doing ALL the chores. He is making sure that she isn't doing too much and he is taking good care of her.

The truth is, Wes stopped doing any of the chores in just a few weeks. From that point on, he only did things after Shirley begged him to and then he wasn't happy about doing it.

Shirley is having a hard time accepting her limitations and it is hard for her to ask for help. In only a few months and after the house begins to look like a pig sty, Shirley can't take it anymore and tells Wes they need to talk about the house.

Shirley: "Honey, I am feeling unnerved about how the house is looking."

Wes: "What do you mean?"

Shirley: "It is filthy."

Wes: "Oh, for God's sake, Shirley, it is fine."

Shirley: "No, it isn't. The toilets are permanently stained, there is burned on grease on the stove that won't come off, and there is something this smells up the refrigerator. There are cobwebs in every corner of the house and dust is covering everything."

Wes: "You are such a neat freak. You can ask any of our friends and they will tell you that you have OCD. Nobody expects a house to be as clean as you think it should be."

Shirley: "You think my standards are unreasonable?"

Wes: "Yep."

Shirley: "You promised me that you would keep the house just like it was before."

Wes: "Don't you think that is a bit ridiculous?"

Shirley: "No. That is how we have lived for over 20 years. Our house has always been clean and tidy."

Wes: "And you don't think it is that way now?"

Shirley: "No."

Wes: "Nobody in the world can ever please you, Shirley. You are way too fussy."

Shirley: "It completely bothers me to see the house this dirty and you keep telling me no to do anything, but you are following through on our agreement."

Wes: "Why do you always have to be so mean? You should listen to yourself. I wish I had a recording to play back to you of the way you talk to me."

Shirley: "Fine, never mind."

Wes: "That's right. Clam up like you always do. Why do you always get to end the discussion? You are mean. I'm going upstairs."

Wes' identity of himself is one where he needs to meet all of Shirley's needs and it isn't a realistic one. Wes doesn't want to admit that he isn't perfect. He likes making agreements that are based on his idealized self. He tells everybody that he is Superman, and there is that tiny part that truly believes him. When his ego mirror, Shirley, doesn't show him as perfect, then he attacks her. This has been going on for over 22 years. Shirley has learned ways to avoid conflict. If she just does all the chores, doesn't complain, then there won't be any problems and Wes can go on believing that he is perfect.

Let's say that Wes has been journaling to stop his codependency. After he storms out, he takes some time to experiment with a mindfulness exercise. By doing this, he sees his behavior and doesn't make any harsh judgments. Because Shirley's self-esteem isn't at stake, he asks himself what he needs to do differently. Is there any way he can stop being so defensive and allow Shirley to feel the way she feels? How could he respond as a partner who is in a relationship that is interdependent? He knows he dropped the ball with the chores, and he does feel guilty. Wes made Shirley admit that she messed up instead of Wes messing up. Wes gets mad at Shirley instead of acting like a partner who truly cares. Shirley is Wes' ego mirror. Wes attacks Shirley and walked out. Is this the type of partner that he truly wants to be? Wes writes in his journal about this and goes back downstairs to talk with Shirley.

Wes: "Home, I am truly sorry about the house. You are absolutely right. I know I've said there isn't anything I wouldn't do for you, but I have dropped the ball on the chores. I know you too well to know that this upsets you a lot."

Shirley starts to cry: "I should have said something sooner before the house got so bad. I expect too much because it is hard for me because I am so weak now."

Wes: "I want you to know you aren't expecting too much, but I might not be able to keep my end of the agreement in a way that will make you happy. What if I pay for somebody to come in a few times a week to clean? I promise to pick up all the dirty clothes and do the laundry. I just can't seem to find the time to do everything else."

Shirley: "That sounds great. Maybe we could even find some time to go to the beach?"

Wes: "I would love that."

Stop Looking In The Mirror

This journaling exercise is going to help you turn away from your ego mirror. Your goal is to allow your ego mirror to quit their job. Let them be themselves, have their own feelings, reactions, and beliefs. It is going to be painful for this person to do time because they are a prisoner of your codependency. They can't be honest. They constantly walk on eggshells just waiting for you to have another meltdown or blow up. There isn't any way they can be rein when they are around you. Due to this, you tow can't have a relationship that is based on interdependency.

Write in your journal every day about your feelings and thoughts. Draw a line down the center of the page. Write down your codependent self-talk. Now you will counter that with interdependent self-talk. You have to know what the deepest problem you have to fix it. Because you are working on your identity, it is going to be worth all the work.

Make an account each day of your codependent feelings and thoughts. Then you have to counter with interdependent thoughts. Here is an example:

- Codependent

  - Why in the world did he get so mad? Yes, I forgot to put the power bill in the mailbox. I didn't do it on purpose. He is just too rigid. He is a jerk.

  - She is overreacting. Why does she get upset about every little thing?

  - How could they be that mean? I worked for hours on that dinner and he didn't say anything about it. He will eat beans from now on.

  - They are never satisfied with anything. I fold the laundry wrong. I bathe the children and did it wrong. I have had it with their criticism.

- Interdependent

- I said I would mail the payment for the power bill and I forgot. I'm not perfect but I do need to apologize and find ways to learn how to be more responsible. I would love for him to be able to count on me. Maybe I could begin writing things down.

- She was extremely upset. I should have helped with the dishes. I should step up and stop being so blind to everything.

- I can tell he is enjoying the dinner, but I need to hear it. I'll just ask him if he likes the chicken.

- They have a problem with being a perfectionist. I like how I do things. Being a good dad and partner is up to me and I am very proud of myself.

It is fundamental to work on this part of codependency. The main goal is to know yourself and stop letting others define who you are. Use emotions to explore yourself. Big deal, your partner got angry just because you didn't do something the way they like it done or they do it. It got done and that is all that matters. This doesn't mean you did something wrong. Even if you did it wrong, this doesn't make you bad. Let your partner feel the way they need to. Acknowledge their feelings and move on. You are still fine.

Set Boundaries

You know there is a difference in how codependents think they should be and the real them with all their flaws. Due to this, a codependent person isn't always going, to be honest. They might make promises that are unrealistic because they think they should and not because they want to. They don't think it is fine for them to ever say no.

With time, deep codependency could become an unending cycle. You may hear things like:

- "If I were a better neighbor, I would help."

- "If I were a good husband, I would spend my weekends fixing the house."

- "If I were a good son, I would ask my parents to move in with me,"

- "If I were a good dad, I would get a loan to pay for my child's tuition."

It isn't possible to be everything to everyone all the time. Because of this, a codependent will let people down and this, in turn, makes others angry. To their horror, they are then seen badly and this reinforces their poor self-esteem.

Moving On From a Codependent Relationship

In some instances, a person must simply get out of a codependent relationship. Whether it's due to physical abuse (which no person should ever be subjected to, period), one party's unwillingness to change, or simply because you've had enough and no longer even wish to be in the relationship any longer, you may find yourself in the situation of having to leave a codependent relationship.

Usually it's fear that keeps a person in an unhealthy relationship. Either you're fearful of being alone or feel obligated to stay in order to maintain your partner's happiness; either way, these are not healthy reasons for staying with someone.

Staying in a codependent relationship that's unfixable for whatever reason is an almost certain way to sabotage your mental, or even physical, wellbeing. Perhaps the codependency has gone so far that it's reached the point at which you feel comfortable experiencing constant emotional pain. If that's the case, and you've concluded that the relationship is past the point of improvement, you must get out.

Unfortunately, people are typically pushed to their breaking points before they can recognize the fact that they must get out of the relationship. Typically, a partner's actions lead to the codependent experiencing a sense of anger. You've been hurt in a way that you didn't think was possible, or perhaps you've been fed up for far too long. Most likely, this awakening will come in the form of anger.

What you have to do, then, is recognize this anger. Although it's a negative emotion, it will fuel your ability to reclaim your self-worth after you've constantly given so much of yourself away for so long.

Because codependency generally stems from a lack of establishing boundaries, it's essential to hone in on this sense of anger. Here's why: anger instinctually encourages you to raise your boundaries. Your natural defense is to reestablish your sense of self, by realizing that you *are* a person with valid feelings and thoughts that have been disregarded.

Of course, recognizing your anger does *not* mean that you should act irrationally, violently, or cruelly. It's simply a means of recognizing the fact that you must preserve your wellbeing and livelihood.

Ending a relationship is almost always difficult. Especially for codependents, it requires a great deal of strength and courage, as well as resolve. Here are some things to keep in mind when ending a codependent relationship:

- Don't just lay all the blame on one party. You don't have to *take* any blame, either, but remember that pointing fingers at this point in your relationship is senseless. Unfortunately, the truth is that codependency is created by a combination of both parties' behaviors.

- Be direct about why you're leaving. Tell the other individual how and why you feel that you've been wronged.

- Don't seek revenge, or purposely try to hurt the other person. Regardless of how hurt you may be feeling, it will only cause you both to feel more pain if you try to be destructive at the end of your relationship.

Once you've left the relationship, you'll need to reestablish your own living space. Whether you get a place of your own or your partner leaves, make your living space individualistic by decorating and arranging things the way *you* see fit.

Following that, you must reclaim your own sense of self-worth. Rediscover the hobbies or activities that you once enjoyed, or seek new ones. Spend time with family and friends, but make sure to set aside some time just for you.

While you may be a bit fragile when you first leave a codependent relationship, keep in mind that things will only improve as time goes on. You'll become stronger and more independent. In order to do so, however, you must be willing to change a bit on your own, as well.

For one thing, try to banish negativity by remembering to be kind to yourself. Don't judge yourself so harshly, and instead, praise yourself for all of the goals (however small they may seem) that you've accomplished.

Also, try to be welcoming when it comes to accepting help from others. Seek strong, caring individuals who genuinely want to see you succeed and support your goal of fostering healthy relationships.

Finally, if and when you find yourself ready to move on and seek a new relationship, truly take the time to assess your feelings. Don't settle just out of fear of being alone - before looking for a partner, think about what your needs are in a relationship. What qualities do you look for in a partner? How can you make sure that your needs are met? Remind yourself that you deserve love and happiness, but keep in mind that you, first and foremost, are responsible for your own happiness. Create happiness, self-worth, and self-love, and then you can move on to create a loving relationship with another.

Healing After a Codependent Relationship

The end of a relationship can be painful for anyone. More so for people whose entire sense of self-worth, identity and validation is dependent on a relationship. Rejection in romantic relationships can be extremely hurtful. It stings our most primal and evolutionary role of reproducing and surviving as a familial unit. Isolation, abandonment and loneliness are often our worst nightmares. While even emotionally healthy people displaying balanced behaviour find it difficult to cope with rejection, it can shatter the world of a codependent.

Break-ups induce a deep sense of grief in codependents. In most cases, it is automatically connected to parental abandonment in their childhood. Codependents often get into a relationship seeking unconditional love to compensate for childhood wounds and unsatisfied desires. They start experiencing feelings of unworthiness and rejection at the slightest trigger in the course of the relationship. The feelings of disdain that they harbour about themselves are so powerful that they even seem to invite or provoke others to treat them similarly. When we feel rejected or inadequate about ourselves, we're encouraging people to reject us and are ultimately caught in the unfortunate "cycle of abandonment" that leads to more fear, insecurity, shame and rejection. We can break out of this cycle by acknowledging our past issues and living in the present.

For best results and faster healing, start making gradual but definite changes to your thoughts and behaviour patterns. Forge a strong relationship with yourself before you jump into another relationship. It may seem extremely painful in the beginning, but contacting your partner will only make your codependency worse. Avoid short terms gains and think about the bigger picture. Think about the wonderful transformation that awaits you if you resist the urge to slip back into your codependent relationship.

Codependents breaking away from unhealthy relationships may experience similar withdrawal symptoms as an addict trying to keep away from the object of their addiction. It can often lead to compulsive behaviour and obsessive thoughts. However, the good news is that there are several ways to heal from a codependent relationship if you acknowledge the condition and work consciously towards dealing with it. Here are some simple yet highly effective ways of healing after a traumatic codependent relationship.

Avoid maintaining any contact with your ex.

Stop texting, calling and sending seemingly harmless feelers out to your ex. It may give you some sort of relief for the time being. However, you're only reinforcing your obsessive-compulsive thoughts and behaviour patterns by keeping yourself tied to the toxic relationship. If you're filing for a legal separation, let it go through a proper and professional channel. Any messages can be communicated through your legal representatives.

Forgive yourself and the other person.

Don't hold grudges against yourself or the other person. Don't be bogged down by feelings of guilt and shame for all that you've endured in the relationship. Gradually, let go of all the feelings and forgive. Forgive yourself and the other person for your own sake. This will free up the space in your mind to be overtaken by more positive thoughts and feelings.

Challenge your negative self-beliefs and false assumptions.

Avoid all negative self-talk such as "I am a loser" or "I don't deserve to be loved" or "I am damaged goods." These negative reinforcements won't do you any good post break-up. On the other hand, work hard to build your self-esteem and self-confidence.

Establish boundaries with your ex.

This is especially important if you're co-parenting with your former partner. Set clear co-parenting rules. Don't be over-accommodating, helpless or aggressive in your interactions. Learn to be assertive and state your needs and preferences in a balanced manner.

Write letters addressed to your ex but don't mail them.

Write letters to your ex without mailing them simply to vent out and express all your feelings. It can be an opportunity for you to admit certain feelings that you were unable to express earlier. Being able to say how you feel without fear of recrimination or hostility can be cathartic. This will invariably assist in clearing up all the negative emotions left over from the relationship, which can be extremely helpful in the healing process. It may just be the closure you need.

Avoid triggers.

It may be tempting to visit places you frequented with your ex-partner, or listen to songs that remind you of times spent together. But these will trigger strong feelings and 'love memories', which can drag you back into the cycle of codependency and create a yearning to return to the relationship. You may do these things to feel a sense of connection with your ex, but it will only lead to more feelings of pain, despair and helplessness and at the very worst case will lead you right back to a codependent relationship you have fought so hard to escape from.

Create a positive aura around you.

Fill up your space with positivity by playing healing chants, lighting up aromatic candles, using essential oils and using symbols that make you feel good about yourself. Meditate to healing chants, practice self-love exercises such as positive self-talk, journaling and visualization.

Don't neglect childhood trauma.

Codependency is often closely correlated to our childhood traumas. Emotional isolation or abandonment in childhood may create a marked need to be accepted by people at any cost. Codependents often harbour negative feelings of neglect, betrayal, abuse, rejection and more. The traumas are deeply ingrained in their subconscious to direct their actions. Sometimes, we are so subconsciously conditioned to think and behave the way we do that we don't even recognize it as abnormal or unhealthy. We just don't know any other way. If you find yourself being a part of unhealthy codependent relationships consistently, revisit your childhood experiences consciously to understand the source of these behaviour patterns. Acknowledging childhood issues and actively seeking help to come to terms with them is a brilliant first step for getting rid of codependency. You can try therapy or counselling to help you overcome childhood issues.

Lock in a plan.

Your best chance for bringing about lasting changes in your life is to commit yourself to a workable plan. Come up with realistic, specific and actionable ways of dealing with certain situations when they arise. Once you've drawn up these plans, you'll find yourself less likely to give in to temptation. Have effective *if this, then that* plans in place. Say for instance, you know you will experience loneliness several times after the break-up. Have a plan ready for times when you feel lonely and are tempted to call your ex. This default destructive mind-set can be sufficiently altered to a more productive one, where you call a friend instead or listen to an empowering song. The more you master this art of doing dealing with situations in a different and controlled way; the more powerful and in control you will feel about your ability to be finally free of unhealthy relationships.

Write enriching and empowering notes to yourself.

This is a remarkable way to come to terms with all your unexpressed and unmet feelings and emotions, and overcome your relationship addiction. You can write elaborate memos to yourself expressing your most fragile moments or feelings that need reinforcement. It can be something such as: "You don't feel up to it now, but you should really make some fun weekend plans with friends." Such encouraging and gently nudging words can guide you to take action without being too hard on yourself. Personal note writing is a pleasant and affirming conversation with yourself that seeks to boost your self-esteem and prompts you to act in a positive way.

Reward yourself for milestones reached.

The post break-up codependency cycle has various stages through which you experience a range of emotions. Reward yourself for crossing each stage that takes you a step ahead towards freedom from an unhealthy relationship. For every conscious act of staying away from the relationship, treat yourself with something fun. It can be a cup of your favourite coffee or a trip to the beach or the best pizza in town. If you've successfully said "no" more than once, pamper yourself with the frozen dark chocolate dessert you've been craving.

Consider undergoing a medical evaluation if the mourning persists.

Though some amount of withdrawal symptoms and mourning is normal, persistent depression can be extremely unhealthy for the body and mind. If you find the continued depression hampering your daily activities, consider making an appointment with your doctor for an evaluation. Among other things, you may be put on an anti-depressants course or put in touch with specialist support.

If you're having trouble in moving on from a codependent relationship, consider attending some Codependents Anonymous group meetings.

You can get lots of information, guidance and support from others who have been through similar experiences, while having an opportunity to interact and make new connections. You will derive confidence from the fact that you aren't the only one suffering from the condition and there are several others like you who are successfully battling it. There are several online discussion forums and helpful chats for people looking to heal from a codependent relationship.

The Habits of Codependent Individuals

- **Please people at their own expense**

Codependents are people-pleasers, that is, they try their best to satisfy the needs and wants of everybody around them. They are always the first to respond to calls for help. The "hero" chromosome in them always pushes them to the front queue of helpers and saviors whenever one is needed. They have an intense need to provide help, and they feed it upon the problems of their friends and family members. Often though, they provide help and care at their own expense. They go the extra lengths even if it means getting burned to make themselves indispensable to anybody that might require help

- **Discomfort with receiving attention or help from others**

Unfortunately, codependents do have scruples with asking for and receiving help. They have been conditioned to keep their emotions and needs close to their chest while growing up and cannot bring themselves to show what they see as weakness. Therefore, they suffer in silence. They don't ask for help and would rather brave the waters on their own. When they receive help such as cash gifts or an unsought for recommendation, they get discomfited and confused about how to react. Therefore, they keep themselves in positions where people don't even know they require help. They may even cover up their lack with an apparent projection of having in excess. Even from the same partner they are codependent upon, they find it hard to take anything apart from appreciation and more requests for help.

- **See themselves from the eyes of other people**

Codependents are some of the most self-critical individuals on earth. Their lack of self-esteem means they are forever insecure and wary of other people's opinions and perception of them. As such, they may out up a fake lifestyle to impress people while remaining essentially hollow inwards. They do not react to negative criticism well and may either respond aggressively or go out of their way to avoid criticism entirely. Most importantly to them though, they are obsessed with how their partner views them. Does he see them as totally indispensable? Are they the only port of call when he runs into trouble again? These are the most important questions that run through the minds of codependents.

- **Conveniently ignore red flags**

Especially in their relationships, codependent individuals always seem not to see the obvious signs. Largely inspired by their dependence on their partners and a reluctance to rock the boat or avoid conflict, they avoid fixing problems within their relationships until it is too late. They keep glossing over warning signs and refuse to heed warnings and obvious hints.

- **Rationalize the mistakes of others**

This is the crux of codependency after all. They are always there with a readymade excuse as to why their partner isn't up to social standards. Alcoholism? Well, he had a troubled childhood. Gambling addiction? He doesn't really gamble that much. Besides, he is rich. Their library of excuses never gets exhausted. Even when the partner obviously recognizes that he has a problem that needs to be solved, they would rather remind him they are there rather than join hands to find a lasting solution.

- **Give more than they receive in relationships**

It is constant in codependent relationships that one party gives out more care, attention and affection than the other. Individuals suffering from codependency constantly subdue the voice of their own needs, do not demand for much if anything at all and are too afraid to speak out their minds. Therefore, it is not surprising to see them constantly giving out more than they receive. Anyways, most of the time, their partners may have "bigger problems" that cries out for their attention than taking stock of the attention they receive.

- **Have loosely defined boundaries**

Boundaries are important in every relationship. They are necessary to ensure that you don't get trampled upon. There has to be limits beyond which you won't go or tolerate. Your friends, family members and partners have to pay you some respect and not overstep their bounds. A boundary helps you mark a fine line to divide your finances, feelings, emotions and needs from that of your partner. Unfortunately, codependent relationships have undefined, poorly defined or blurred boundaries. Partners see themselves as an extension of the other half. There are no limits and invariably, emotions and desires get trampled upon. Codependents do not set boundaries because they want to remain open and be the first port of call for as many people as people when crises arise.

- **Say yes all the time**

A codependent does not know or use the word "NO" to any request. He never opts out of giving a service if he can, no matter the lengths he has to go to provide it. This doesn't mean that he is totally comfortable with all tasks though. He has just been configured to make himself inconvenient before he thinks of disappointing any other person. Against the backdrop of a childhood most likely spent seeking the good graces and approval of difficult parents and probably unyielding siblings, it is easy to understand why the thoughts of turning down a request might be so foreign to a codependent individual.

- **Feelings of guilt or responsibility for the suffering of others**

The initial phase of codependency stems from a heightened sense of responsibility and duty to help other people overcome their sufferings. Especially for people who became codependent as a result of having to cater to the needs of an ill friend or relation, they become filled with the idea that they are the only ones in a unique position to help every other person around them. Therefore, they feel heavy guilt when they are unable to stem the tide of suffering that an associate is experiencing. They see it as a failure when they are not considered to help alleviate suffering or when their ministrations fail to yield positive results. They therefore relax their boundaries and limits lower to further cater for others. Their show of care is the only thing that gives them joy and satisfaction and when people suffer, it raises a sense of guilt in them.

- **Reluctance to share true thoughts or feelings for fear of displeasing others**

Children who grow up to be codependent are taught not to show emotions or admit weaknesses. They grow into adults incapable of intimacy. Intimacy in this instance does not refer to sexual activity although it has also been found to be affected. Intimacy in this context refers to the ability to share their feelings, emotions and desires with their partners and be capable of demanding for their rights as equal partners. Scared of displeasing people or thinking they may offend people by asking for help, they keep their true feelings within them and play to the gallery.

Why You Should Not Be Codependent

Codependency is a dangerous trait to possess. Life has evolved at a blinding stage and our society right now is on the fast pace. We get bombarded daily with opinions, requests, offers of friendship and disappointments that it becomes simply too dangerous to tie your life inextricably with anybody else's own. What are the specific dangers that codependency may bring into your life;

- **Kills off self-esteem and confidence**

Allison Pescosolido writes, "Nothing erodes self-esteem quicker than an unhealthy relationship". When you hitch your happiness to a need to be needed, you soon begin to forget that you have self-worth. Codependency teaches you that your life isn't worth much beyond that of your partner. Codependents think only of their partners and new ways in which they may care for him. You lose your own sense of direction and your work may even begin to suffer. Worst of all, a lot of dependents take advantage of your urge and consistently berate and force you to do acts that further shatter what little self-confidence you possess. Codependents may even suffer constant sexual and physical abuse and yet, believe they simply can't exist outside the realm of their partner's need and affection. There is a voice at the back of their head telling them they are just an extension of their partners. They constantly need to seek approval and acknowledgement from their partners and derive lesser joy from their personal achievements.

- **Turns you antisocial**

The inherent need to seek approval and feel loved makes codependents decidedly antisocial. Codependency can easily turn you into a social recluse outside your partner's presence. Feeling insecure and decidedly unable to assess if their efforts are worth extra praise, codependents often turn to staying off social encounters. They miss engagements with other people, can be quite boring and unable to focus on conversations and generally exhibit a wide range of actions that suggests they would rather be left alone.

- **Relegates your own goals**

A codependent individual may be genuinely successful. He may break records, achievements and produce huge strides in the corporate and business world but deep down, codependency often leaves a yawning gap in their hearts. No matter the scale of your achievements, codependency teaches you to cherish the needs of your partners above every other goal. As such, you may find yourself unable to commit the same amount of resources and drive to attaining personal business. Codependents have been known to give up their work and life goals to focus on a partner with needs such as alcoholism. Codependency takes away your goals and makes your partner the sole center of your existence.

- **A helpless mindset**

Codependency makes you feel and act helpless. Codependent individuals become chained down by the weight of the expectations they have placed on their own heads. They develop a feeling of helplessness in the face of their relationship struggles. They hang on to their relationships because they can't seem to see any other option. They suffer neglect and abuse and still remain steadfast in their relationships because codependency tells them they have no option. An even worse aspect is that they see their partners as having no control over their actions. They treat their partners like children that have no control over what they do. They help them make excuses of not being in total control.

- **Can affect your health severely**

Codependency can be a health threat. Anxiety, depression and stress are three major psychological disorders currently on the rise worldwide, and depending on another individual to provide you joy and relief is a short path to overloading your circuit. By taking on too much worries and making themselves open to so many problems, codependents pile more stress onto themselves and this can easily escalate into depression and anxiety disorders. Insomnia is also never too far away from most codependents.

- **Leaves you firmly vulnerable to emotional injury**

Once you have taken control of your life and handed it over to somebody else's actions and inactions, you have set yourself up to be at his mercy. He/she can hurt you even unknowingly with the smallest of actions and you become extra sensitive to being hurt in any case. Opinions and criticism from any quarter also sting more. Your deprecated sense of self-worth and low esteem could also leave you in delicate quarters when it comes to emotions and feelings.

- **Makes you open to picking up bad habits and addictions**

Emotional injury and a loss of esteem aren't the only dangers that can arise from overdependence. A soft spot for a partner who has addiction problems could turn you into an enabler who helps him satisfy his addiction as a means of keeping him pleased. Even worse still, you could pick up the same bad habits in the hope of keeping him company. Addictions such as gambling, alcoholism and substance abuse can be easily picked up especially when your friend or partner already has a steady source. By becoming codependent on him, you could end up picking the same habits.

- **Refusing help from other people**

One of the primary demerits of codependency is the way it draws you back from seeking help yourself. Codependents are so enmeshed in a control complex that they totally adore being in control and would not admit to things being skewed with them too. They grow to be emotionally flat and cannot bring themselves to show any form of emotion. They learn to exist independently of any help from the people around them and lose the ability to ask for proper help.

- **A victim's mindset**

Codependents constantly feel cheated at all times. Their mind is a hodge-podge of conflicting emotions and they end up feeling underappreciated a lot of times. Codependency does not allow them pick faults with their partners and instead, they turn against the system. They help sympathize with their partners and teach them to look for conspiracy theories to absolve their partners of their misdeeds.

- **Stresses you out physically and mentally**

The human body has a threshold for the amount of problems and issues it can take at once. By adding more problems and issues outside of your own to your mind, you run the risk of maxing out your resilience and capability to withstand stress. Obviously, catering for a partner's needs will leave you with extra physical activity to carry out. Partners with problems such as chronic illness or alcoholism may need constant care that may task your physical capabilities beyond its limits. Of even more severe potentials is the risk of a mental overload. Piling up too many worries in your head can deal dangers to your psyche.

EMPATH

Introduction

Empaths have a better understanding of energy than they do the words that are coming out of a person's mouth. This is one of the reasons you can't lie to an empath—they will sense it. Empaths can listen to someone speaking a language they don't understand but have full insight into what they are trying to express based on their energy. Empaths listen to words, pay attention to body language, and translate energetic vibrations. They are especially vulnerable to negativity because it takes from their energy field. On the other hand, when empaths are surrounded by positive energy, they become relaxed and their aura expands in an outward direction as their feelings and emotions flow freely without tension. Positive energy is like a charger—it boosts you up and refills you. This is why empaths will avoid conflict at all costs, shut down when confronted with it, and stay away from certain people and places. The body goes into self-defense mode in an attempt to preserve energy so that you don't become tired and exhausted.

Whether you know it or not, empaths can choose who and what influences their energy—they decide where it is sent and to whom. Our thoughts are so powerful that as soon as they are released, anyone capable of tuning in to your frequency will automatically pick them up. In other words, empaths have the ability to read minds. A skilled empath knows how to protect themselves by being fully aware of what is taking place around them and being present so that no one is able to enter their energy field without their permission.

Once you learn how energy works, it is important that you use it wisely. Remember what goes around comes around, and whatever you put out into the world will come right back to you. Energy is like a drug—the more you experiment with it and enjoy the way it makes you feel, the easier it is to become addicted to it. Your energy, if not protected, will abandon you, become reckless, and attach itself to any other energy circulating in the atmosphere. When empaths are alert and aware, they can quickly recognize subtle changes that take place in their environment without needing to use any of their five senses—smell, touch, taste, sight, or hearing.

Once energy has been released, it travels in an outward direction and never dies. It remains in the air and clings to people or objects, and other energies absorb it or connect with it. Our energy leaves a legacy wherever we go, which is why you can step into an environment and immediately pick up on the vibe of it. That vibe is dependent upon the people or the event that is taking place there.

Once you realize that your energy is constantly interacting with other people's energy, regardless of space, time, or distance, it can become overwhelming, and you will feel as though you need to get back to yourself. But this is because society has conditioned us to believe that our mind and body are two separate entities.

What Is An Empath?

Empathy is a form of emotional connection that is accessible to almost everyone on the planet, but an empath is more than simply a person who experiences empathetic feelings. An individual with healthy empathetic sensibilities can use their empathy as a tool when circumstances call for it, but an empath often doesn't have the option of putting that tool away or choosing when, where, and how to apply it. Some empaths see their heightened sensitivity as a gift, but many others find it frustrating and difficult to manage.

Why is it that some people can feel and understand the suffering of others while others cannot? How is it that some people can remain so cold to others to the extent of being indifferent and uncaring while others can envision the problems, empathize, and even look for ways to help them?

Definition of Empathy

Empathy and sympathy are both fluids-these are not fixed traits, but rather skills that can be honed and strengthened, or grow weak from misuse over time. You may go through periods of your life wherein you find it easy to walk past a person in need without a second thought, and yet feel that it's impossible to ignore them at other times. But there is a certain degree of empathic ability that is currently considered standard or average for most humans-we tend to feel stronger empathy in childhood. As adults, we learn to regulate our emotional responses and distinguish them from other people's, deciding when and where it's most appropriate to display empathy, or to keep our feelings to ourselves.

When empathy is present to a useful degree, it is not typically measured, since it is displayed in varied forms from one person to another, and we still do not have commonly agreed upon metrics by which to evaluate it. But we rely on the standard degree of empathy for so many of our interpersonal connections, that most of us tend only to notice when it is missing from an interaction, rather than when it is present, like oxygen. It feels natural to most of us to rearrange our facial muscles and display concern when we face someone who is crying or obviously in distress; therefore, if we note someone is smiling or laughing in response to another person's misery, we can immediately sense that something is "off."

Within the past few decades, the fields of psychology, neuroscience, and many others have made enormous strides in research towards understanding the minds of those who do not display the "normal" amount of empathy. There are some conditions, such as autism or Asperger's syndrome, wherein a person seems able to detect the emotional energies of those around them but lacks the necessary cognitive tools to interpret them or determine an appropriate reaction. These people often feel attacked or overwhelmed when the emotions of others resonate within them, which is a form of empathic sensitivity, but they often react by shutting down or self-isolating rather than trying to find a way to harmonious coexistence. It is not a struggle for these people to put their own needs first in interpersonal connections, even if it is at the expense of other people's feelings, but this isn't a malicious sentiment; it is primarily a self-preservation instinct in hyper-drive.

Alternatively, there are empathy-deficient personality disorders, such as narcissism, sociopathy, and psychopathy, wherein a person is capable of recognizing the emotions of others, but feels personally detached from them. That is why we often describe psychopathic criminals as "cold" or "calculating." It is unsettling to imagine that a person could decide to take action, knowing that their behavior will cause pain or suffering in others and that they might remain unbothered by that factor or derive pleasure from it-but that is the thought process of an empathy-disordered individual. The feelings of others are considered unimportant because they do not impact their emotional sensations.

The general population holds a lot of misconceptions about people with these personality disorders, which are most evident within the criminal justice system. Many of us convince ourselves, for instance, that these people commit crimes of passion, temporarily losing their sense of right and wrong in the blinding heat of rage, or that they are so mentally skewed as to be incapable of understanding how much pain and suffering they are causing. Unfortunately, neither of these possibilities proves true for these individuals. They do understand the impact of their actions and are capable of determining right from wrong, yet they choose to ignore these factors, hurting other people to serve strategic needs or for the sake of personal gain. People with these personality disorders generally display impressive skill with cognitive empathy, which you might think of as theoretical empathy; this allows them to theorize or predict the emotional reactions of others and makes them masterful manipulators.

When discussing those who struggle to display or feel empathy, it's important to remember that empathic abilities are fluid, not fixed in stone; anyone willing to put in the effort can improve their empathic capabilities, even those who have been diagnosed with an empathy deficient condition or disorder. Physical empathy is often accessible to those who do not display emotional empathy, which may be a function of evolutionary development. Humans can better protect their physical bodies by recognizing physical pain in others and are biologically driven to mimic pleasurable behaviors (whether that means eating good food or enjoying sexual stimulation) by watching others and empathizing with their enjoyment of such activities. Since this form of empathy is often observable in scans of empathy-disordered brains, we must embrace the notion that empathy exists as a complex and fluid and scale; it is not like a light switch that is either flipped on or off.

The Source of Empathic Power

The question of where empathic powers come from, or how people come to possess them, is one that science still does not have a solid answer. But there are a few theories. There is indeed plenty of evidence to suggest that a "normal" degree of empathy is accessible to most of us in early development. Newborn infants in neonatal units display an inability to distinguish personal feelings from those around them; if one infant begins to cry, usually most others will follow suit very quickly, as they are not yet aware that this pain or anxiety isn't theirs to own. Most infants who receive a healthy amount of care and attention will continue mimicry and emotional enmeshment throughout the first few years of life-this is how children can learn speech and movement. Some children, raised in especially tight-knit families or communities, may struggle at first to understand the function of pronouns that distinguish between the individual self and the group, posing questions like, "Mama, why are we sad today?" when they observe this emotion in another person.

Those who believe in the supernatural possibilities of empathic power also tend to think that certain individuals are fated to receive these gifts and that empaths feel as they do to serve some higher purpose as determined by cosmic or holy design. This belief often coincides with the notion that empaths are born unique, and not shaped by their surroundings; while the level of power they possess or how they channel energy may fluctuate throughout their lives, their heightened sensitivity is considered an innate trait. Conversely, there are those who believe empathic abilities come from the environment or circumstances in which a person is raised, as a function of nurture rather than nature. Many psychologists note that children raised in volatile, neglectful, or dangerous households learn early on to detect subtle changes in their parents' behaviors as a necessary coping skill and defense mechanism, allowing them to predict, avoid, or even prevent traumatic episodes.

Parents may not necessarily be evil or malicious in raising a child who develops extreme empathic sensitivity. Some theories posit that the only environmental factor needed to trigger such a development is an older authoritative figure in the child's life, which requires the child to empathize with them frequently. For example, a parent who is grieving the loss of a loved one might, without ever intending to, compel their child to empathize with a level of emotional pain which they haven't yet been prepared for, and can hardly even comprehend at such a young age. A child who is put in this position frequently enough may never learn to distinguish their own emotions from those of others, and might even struggle to feel that they are real, substantial, or whole without the influence of another dominant personality. They become hyper-focused on caring for the parental figure in their life, and never learn how to receive care without guilt, shame or anxiety, as most children do.

Whatever you believe, one thing is clear. The empathic ability must be understood, trained, and balanced to be part of a healthy, happy lifestyle. You can evaluate the strength of your empathic sensitivity and determine how much energy to channel into further education, training, and healing.

By now, you may be feeling reasonably confident that you experience empathy with an atypical degree. But to hone and master your empathic skills, you'll need to determine what type of empath you are. Essentially, this is a question of what form of energetic vibration you pick up on the most easily.

Empath And Spiritual Hypersensitive

Empaths often suffer from spiritual based hypersensitivity; the symptoms include:

- Your environment causes you to feel overwhelmed
- Sounds are too loud, even if made at a normal range
- You constantly feel the feelings of others

This type of energetic overwhelm is nothing new; the spiritual community has been dealing with it for many years. As more and more empaths choose to ignore their gift, they are becoming less connected with the universe, which has led to an increase in spiritual based hypersensitivity. Oversensitivity to people's energy and noise is a common reaction to energy acceleration, as you ascend to higher heights in your spiritual development, you should expect to experience this. When you begin to accelerate in the spiritual realm, you may feel like a radio signal picking up a million signals at once. When there is a shift in spiritual vibration, your sense of intuition and your emphatic channels are open causing a heightened awareness of the thoughts and feelings of those around you. Spiritual hypersensitivity can manifest physically causing third eye dizziness, hypersensitivity to energy, odors, light and noise. Metaphysics believes that the body is a vehicle for the spirit, the body is not who we are; our person is carried in our spirit. Wayne Dyer states that we are spiritual beings living in a physical world.

How to Cope With Spiritual Hypersensitivity

When the body is overwhelmed physically, emotionally or mentally, the fight or flight syndrome is activated and breathing becomes shallow. When you begin to experience a change in your breathing pattern, you should immediately start practicing conscious breathing. This is where you focus your attention on your breath, which will slow down your nervous system and allow you to relax. Breathe slowly, deeply and in a rhythm at the same time as focusing your mind on being able to relax in the situation that you are in. You should always take a temporary retreat from any stressful situation such as family or work-related conflicts. Excusing yourself to the bathroom is a good way to do this. This will allow you to get away from the negative energy, practice your breathing techniques and renew yourself.

There are also several spiritual healing tools that you can use:

Water

Water has extraordinary balancing and healing properties during times of hypersensitivity. When consumed with consciousness, it provides inner alignment. You can balance the surrounding energy by putting a drop of water on your third eye area. When you apply water that you have energized, it leads to even more powerful results. You can energize water by praying over it, or putting a word on the bottle with the intention of infusing the words frequency into the bottle. Words such as healing, calmness, and peace work well.

Taking a hot shower works well for aura cleansing and for the restoration of energetic balance. Take a shower and imagine the water washing away negative feelings, impressions and thoughts from others and envision all of the negative energy being sucked down the drain.

Mindfulness

This technique can pull calming energy into the body. Focus on your breath at the same time as looking at something beautiful like a rose, the sun or the sky. You can even focus on the palm of your hands as if this is the first time you have seen them. You can redirect the attention you are paying to your feelings by focusing on something visual.

Essential Oils

Essential oils have a calming effect and can greatly improve the anxiety associated with spiritual hypersensitivity. The American College of Healthcare Sciences conducted a study in 2014, in which 58 hospice patients were given a daily hand massage for one week using a blend of essential oils. The oil blend was made up of lavender, frankincense and bergamot. All patients reported less depression and pain as a result of the essential oil massages. The study concluded that essential oil blend aromatherapy massages were more effective for depression and pain management than massage alone.

The following are some of the best oils for treating anxiety:

Lavender

Lavender oil has a relaxing and calming effect; it restores the nervous system, provides inner peace, better sleep, causes a reduction in restlessness, panic attacks, irritability and general nervous tension. There have been several clinical studies proving that inhaling lavender causes an immediate reduction in anxiety and stress. One study discovered that taking lavender oil capsules orally led to an increase in heart rate variation in comparison to the placebo while watching a film that caused anxiety. The study concluded that lavender had an anxiolytic effect, which means that it has the ability to inhibit anxiety.

Other studies have concluded that lavender has the ability to reduce anxiety in patients having coronary artery bypass surgery and in patients who are afraid of the dentist.

Rose

Rose alleviates depression, anxiety, grieving, shock and panic attacks. The Iranian Red Crescent Medical Journal published a study in which a group of women experiencing their first pregnancy inhaled rose oil for 10 minutes at the same time as having a footbath. A second group of women experiencing pregnancy for the first time was also given the footbath but without the rose oil inhalation. The results discovered that a footbath combined with aromatherapy caused a reduction in anxiety in nulliparous (a woman that has not had any children yet) women in the active phase.

Vetiver

Vetiver oil contains reassuring, grounding and tranquil energy. It is often used for patients experiencing trauma and helps with stabilization and self-awareness. It also has a calming effect. Vetiver oil is a nervous system tonic; it reduces hypersensitivity, jitteriness, shock and panic attacks. The Natural Product Research published a study that examined rats with anxiety disorders and found that vetiver oil caused a reduction in anxiety.

Chamomile

Chamomile oil is known for its calming effect and its ability to produce inner peace, reduce worry, anxiety, over-thinking and irritability. The University of Pennsylvania School of Medicine conducted an explorative study and found that it contains medicinal anti-depressant properties. The National Center for Complementary and Integrative Health also found that chamomile capsules have the ability to reduce anxiety related symptoms.

Frankincense

Frankincense oil is great for treating anxiety and depression due to its tranquil energy and calming effects. It also helps you focus, quiet the mind and deepen meditation. A Keimyung University study in Korea found that a combination of lavender, frankincense and bergamot reduced pain and depression in hospice patients suffering from terminal cancer.

How to Use Essential Oils for Hypersensitivity

Essential oils are either ingested, applied topically or used in aromatherapy. Here are some suggestions for their usage:

Aromatherapy

Aromatherapy is a very popular remedy for anxiety because of the human ability to process information through smell; it can trigger a very powerful emotional response. There is a region in the brain called the limbic system that controls memory recall and emotional processing. Inhaling the scent of essential oils stimulates a mental response in the brain's limbic system, which regulates stress and calming responses such as the production of hormones, blood pressure and breathing patterns. You can use the oils in the bath, a hot water vapor, direct inhalation, a humidifier or vaporizer, cologne, perfume, a vent or aromatherapy diffusers.

Oral Application

You can consume the majority of essential oils orally. However, it is essential that the oils you use are safe and pure. The majority of commercialized oils have been blended with synthetics or diluted with other substances making them unsafe for ingesting. The most effective method for consuming essential oils is to combine a drop of oil with a teaspoon of honey or drop the oil into a glass of water. You can also add a couple of drops to the food you are cooking.

Topical Application

Topical application is the process of placing essential oils on the skin, nails, teeth, hair or mucous membranes of the body. The oils are quickly absorbed by the skin. Due to the strength of the oils, it is essential that you dilute or blend them with a carrier oil such as coconut, avocado, jojoba, or sweet almond oil. You can apply the blended mixture directly to the affected area, around the rims of the ears, the soles of the feet, in the bath, through a warm compress, or through a massage.

How To Protect Yourself From Energy Vampires

Have you ever gone somewhere feeling vibrant and after spending time around that place, you felt drained of energy? Or have you ever met someone and after spending time with them, you felt an energy drain? Both of these situations point to an encounter with an energy vampire. Most energy vampires are only interested in their own desires, lack empathy, and are incredibly immature. An energy vampire will leave you feeling exhausted, irritated, and overwhelmed. An energy vampire can be anyone – friends, family, coworkers, etc. Once you realize that someone is a vampire, you should do yourself a favor and cut them off from your life. Getting rid of an energy vampire is not a self-serving deed; it is an act of self-preservation. The vibrations of energy, vampires are incredibly low. As a coping strategy, they have to suck energy from others through the following ways:

Gossiping: An energy vampire knows that people want to hear a good story. So, they say anything in an attempt to earn the attention of their victim. They resort to telling lies about people. If an energy vampire tells you about other people, you can be sure that they will tell other people about you as well. They also start slow wars between factions by telling each side antagonizing news.

Manipulation: An energy vampire is a master manipulator. Before they approach anyone, they already have a script to play by and have rehearsed how to take advantage of that person. They have no remorse about manipulating people into doing their bidding, as their capacity to empathize is incredibly limited. Energy vampires get a high out of manipulating people and getting their way.

Complaining: No one is more "wronged" in the entire world. An energy vampire believes that the world is out to get them. They can take advantage of someone and yet find a way of twisting the story so that they appear to be the victims. An energy vampire is good at weaving stories together, and they have the experience of passing themselves off as victims. Due to this habit of complaining, an energy vampire tends to be slack in their work, knowing too well they can find something to complain about or someone to throw the blame at.

Massive ego: An energy vampire has a massive ego, and it comes with delusions of grandeur. An energy vampire sets themselves extremely ambitious goals. The goals are unrealistic because they lack the wherewithal of achieving these goals. Their massive ego also manifests in how they treat other people. Energy vampires think that they are special people and are above everyone else. Thus, they act self-entitled and expect everyone to bow down to them. When an energy vampire comes into your life, they will normally have an agenda of taking something away from you, before they move on to the next victim.

Not being accountable: An energy vampire will hardly ever be accountable for anything. They want easy things and hate responsibility. Due to this hatred of accountability, energy vampires make the worst candidates for doing any serious task. They will usually disappoint you. If you have to rely on an energy vampire for the completion of a task, they will frustrate you with their subpar performance and an unwillingness to be accountable. Energy vampires will develop a hatred toward anyone that expects them to be answerable, but when the shoe is on the other foot, they are extremely ruthless.

Neglecting the needs of their dependents: Energy vampires are only interested in their own needs and woe unto anyone that depends on them. For instance, if the energy vampire in question has a family, they may spend their earnings on vain things like sex and alcohol at the expense of their family. The people that depend on an energy vampire lead very sad lives because of both the cruelty and humiliation that the energy vampire metes out at them. More often than not, children raised by energy vampires turn into social misfits because they have known nothing but pain their whole lives. When an energy vampire is around you, you will feel uneasy, and soon your energy levels will take a massive dip. The following are some things that take place when attacked by an energy vampire:

Nausea: After an interaction with an energy vampire, you can be left feeling nauseous. This feeling may be accompanied by a stomach ache. This happens because your body is going through a lot of stress because of losing energy. Once you get rid of the energy vampire, both the nausea and the stomach ache will go away.

Headache: An energy vampire will also make you experience a terrible headache. Once your energy levels go down, there's not enough energy for your brain. The brain reacts by trying to create awareness of the fact that the body has run out of sugars. The brain consumes a significant portion of the total energy of a person, and if the energy suffers a drop, a person's ability to use their mental faculties is severely affected.

Once you find out that someone is an energy vampire, the ultimate remedy is to cut the person out of your life. However, in some instances, you're stuck with them because they play an indispensable role in your life. The following are tips to help you cope against attacks from energy vampires:

Set boundaries: Let the person know that you have boundaries that are not to be crossed. This limits the time that you get to spend around the energy vampire.

Recite positive mantras: Mantras are short phrases that a person says over and over with the intention of reaffirming a particular belief. Create more positive energy for yourself by reciting mantras.

Visualization: Using your mind's eye, visualize a membrane of light around your body, shielding your energy from loss. This will greatly reduce the amount of energy lost to the vampire.

Living As An Empath

A highly sensitive person has an intense cognitive processing toward emotional, mental, and physical stimuli. This makes them react to things in different ways than well-adjusted people. The following are some traits that highly sensitive people exhibit:

Easily overwhelmed

A highly sensitive person is easily overwhelmed by different stimuli. For instance, they can't handle staying in environments with too much noise or light. They are sensitive to the extra noise and light. Sensitive people like establishing familiarity with things first before they start using them habitually. This makes them appear odd in front of other well-adjusted people.

Take a lot of time to complete tasks

It can be a real nightmare for a sensitive person to be required to complete a task within a limited amount of time. Sensitive people like taking their time when performing a task. Their mental activity is vigorous. Their thoughts shoot off in a dozen ways, and they have a hard time reconciling the fact that they have to deliver perfect results and time is limited. Sensitive people can hardly perform when they are subjected to a lot of pressure. For this reason, they do well in artistic careers like designing than high-pressure careers like news reporting.

They like staying alone

The average person likes to mix with other people in order not to feel alone. However, a sensitive person likes staying alone. This doesn't mean that they close off human ties altogether. They might keep a small group of friends for their socializing needs. Sensitive people like retreating into solitude because they get drained when they spend time with others. They can perceive the thoughts and energies of other people around them and actually soak up these energies. Their ability to absorb other peoples' energies forces them to isolate themselves so that they don't have to go through that again.

Extremely observant

The average person only ever sees the obvious. For instance, when the average person walks into their boss' office, they might take notice of only their dress style. However, a sensitive person would go deeper into the subtleties. They would notice the color of the clothes, the type of shoes, the angle of the boss's eyes, the smell, and so on. Sensitive people have sharp observation skills. They are the first to notice an anomaly or notice a deviation from the norm.

Cannot function well when over-aroused

A sensitive person has to first get over their arousal before they can function in a normal way. For instance, if they receive extremely elating news, they are forced to stop doing whatever they are doing and concentrate on celebrating. They can only go back to the right headspace for work once they have gotten over the exciting news. If a sensitive person were forced to work while they were in an aroused state, they'd surely not perform. To minimize such cases, sensitive people have to get rid of things that may stimulate them when they are supposed to be busy.

Can read the minds and moods of other people

The average, well-adjusted person can hardly read the mind of other people, but a sensitive person would only have to glance at a person, and they'd read their mind. This special ability helps them anticipate what other people are about to say or do – and in most cases, they are right. Sensitive people are very intuitive, and they rely on this gift to detect the vibrations of those around them. Thus, they can read not only other peoples' minds but moods too.

Very imaginative

A sensitive person has a childlike sense of wonder inside them. They are always poring through things in their minds. Banking on their wealth of emotions, a sensitive person has a rich imagination which they tap into when needed. A sensitive person is far more likely to come up with a creative solution to a problem than a non-sensitive individual. Their creativity makes them suitable for careers in the arts. They tend to flourish where there are no conventional rules, and there's permission to express oneself as their imagination dictates.

Very philosophical

Sensitive people tend to ask deep, philosophical questions. The world presents this huge mystery, and they have to try to understand the world through a philosophical perspective. A sensitive person will have questions, such as where did humans come from? Why are we here? What is our destiny? Their philosophical mind stretches from wanting to find answers about human existence to all other aspects of life. They may have a philosophy touching upon sexuality, society, and the education system. Sensitive people also tend to read a lot in an attempt to explain away their deep unanswered questions.

Comprehend human emotions better than other people
Human emotions can be quite confusing. The average person may not be able to understand their own emotions or the emotions of other people. It doesn't matter how these emotions are well explained; you may find yourself not fully comprehending the depth or nature of a person's emotions. However, when it comes to a sensitive person, they are very good at decoding the exact feelings of a person. Sometimes, they don't even have to be told, as they can deduce for themselves by just looking at what the person in question has been through. For instance, if someone's parents have been murdered, the person will obviously go into mourning. However, a sensitive person can perceive precisely how devastated the person feels.

Can stay still for long periods of time

A sensitive person can stay still for an extended period of time provided there are no distractions. This ability allows them to be incredibly focused when performing a task. But then they don't necessarily have to be working. A sensitive person can plop down onto a seat and stay still for a long period of time without engaging in any activity whatsoever. This is difficult for the average person considering that they need constant human contact.

How Empathy Affects Your Daily Life

Being an empath is something that affects every area of your life. It's not liked a job where you clock in, do your work, clock out and go home. The experience of being an empath is one that takes place 24 hours a day, 7 days a week. Subsequently, there is no area of your life that is left unaffected by your empathic abilities. Although you can't prevent your empathic nature from influencing your life you can manage those influences, thereby taking control from the effects of your emotional environment.

Health

One of the most common areas affected by empathic abilities is a person's health. The negative effects of the constant bombardment of emotions can be overwhelming at best and devastating at worst. Although these effects cannot be avoided altogether when a person is aware of them, they can make decisions and choices that better protect their wellbeing. Some of the lesser physical symptoms that empaths frequently suffer from include headaches, fatigue and minor panic attacks. These are usually brought on by long exposure to large crowds, noisy environments or any other situation involving harsh sensory input. Such symptoms fade quickly once the empath finds a quiet place in which to rebalance their energies. In the event that they cannot get away, these symptoms can turn into more extreme forms, including migraine, dizziness, nausea and even muscle pain.

In addition to affecting physical health and wellbeing, empathic abilities can significantly affect a person's emotional health and wellbeing as well. Lesser symptoms include a general feeling of sadness, low energy levels and even mild stress and anxiety. Such symptoms are usually the result of being in a negative environment or around people with negatively charged emotions. They can also be the result of becoming emotionally spent due to helping those in need. If left unchecked, these symptoms can turn into more serious issues, including depression, extreme anxiety and even rage in some cases. Needless to say, it is critical that you find a place of solitude in the event that you start experiencing any of these symptoms, as only then can you begin to undo the harmful effects of your environment. Daily meditation will also help to increase your stamina in highly charged emotional environments.

Addictions

Many empaths find the constant flow of emotional energy that bombards their senses hard to cope with from time to time. While most find healthy ways to deal with these situations' others turn to less healthy methods. In fact, some develop addictions in their quest to dull their senses and bring a sense of tranquility to their minds. While some addictions are less harmful than others, the bottom line is that no addiction is truly healthy. Therefore, it is important that you be on the lookout for addictive behavior in your life in order to avoid any long-term, harmful consequences.

One such addiction is eating. This makes a lot of sense when you consider the effects food can have on both the body and the mind. Most eating addictions involve treats or comfort food, things that make a person happy just thinking about them. Thus, not only do foods such as ice cream and cake provide a quick boost of sugary energy, they also create a sense of comfort and peace that helps to restore the mind. From time to time such an indulgence can be healthy, however, when that indulgence turns into addiction it can have very negative effects on both body and mind.

Other addictions include drinking alcohol and smoking. These addictions also make sense seeing as they provide a chemical depressant that helps to dull an empath's senses, thereby relieving them from the inner chaos and turmoil that their mind experiences most of the time. Shopping is another common addiction, one that is less understood than the others. However, it makes perfect sense when you take the time to truly consider it. When a person shops they have the hope and expectation of finding something that will bring joy and fulfillment to their lives. Since empaths often suffer from sadness and even depression, such an expectation will go a long way to raising their spirits. In the end, these addictions are usually nothing more than an empath's way of self-medicating through their more serious bouts of depression and anxiety.

If you experience such addictive behavior it is critical to talk to someone who might be able to help you overcome it. Alternatively, turning to such things as meditation and exercise in place of addictive behavior can actually help replace unhealthy habits with healthier, more beneficial ones.

Relationships, Love, And Sex

Unfortunately, the empathic nature of a person often results in them finding themselves in the midst of toxic relationships that they simply cannot escape. Therefore, even when they realize their relationship is toxic, they become stuck as they can't bring themselves to cause suffering to the other person by ending the relationship. Talking to someone, be it a friend or a counselor, can go a long way to resolving this dilemma. Another way that empaths struggle with relationships is that they are often emotionally spent, meaning that they don't always have the energy needed to nurture a healthy and loving relationship. This doesn't mean that empaths don't crave deep and meaningful relationships, rather they don't usually reserve enough emotional energy to invest in their own happiness, spending it all on the happiness of others instead. The only real solution to this is for an empath to find someone who is both very energetic as well as very understanding with regard to the empath's plight.

Love and sex are also highly impacted by a person's empathic abilities. While many people see sex as an act that expresses love between two people, empaths often see it as a way to deaden their senses, restoring them to a state of being physically grounded. This can cause tension in any relationship where the other person feels more lusted after than loved when it comes to intimacy. The truth of the matter is that empaths will never engage in an intimate encounter with anyone who they don't love deeply, therefore any intimate activity will always be done out of love regardless of outward appearances. The important thing for any empath is to make sure they demonstrate their love for their partner on a regular basis through any means possible.

Parenting

Parenting is a challenging enough experience on its own, let alone when it involves an empath at one end or the other. Even so, every empath alive has grown up as a child with empathic abilities, and countless empaths start families of their own, thus entering the world of being a parent with empathic abilities. The increase of emotional awareness between parents and children can be both a blessing and a curse. It is therefore critical that you become aware of the dangers so that you can better manage the effects of your empathic abilities within your family relationships.

As a parent you will struggle with the flow of emotional input you receive from your children. This is made worse by the fact that children are usually full of conflicting and confusing emotions due to the biochemical changes their bodies are constantly going through. Needless to say, this only serves to increase the chaotic nature of the emotional input, creating a never-ending whirlwind in your mind. It is essential that you develop the ability to detach from emotional input in order to protect yourself from becoming completely unhinged as a result of such heightened emotional stimuli. Practicing yoga or meditation on a daily basis can help make all the difference. One of the positives of being an empathic parent is that you can sense when your children are suffering. This gives you an advantage of being able to make yourself available to them even when they are trying to hide their inner turmoil. Taken too far, however, this ability can turn into a form of privacy invasion, therefore only ever use it as a tool, never as a weapon. If your children refuse the help you offer you need to respect their privacy and let them deal with their situation on their own.

As a child you will find life somewhat more difficult because of your empathic abilities. Every child does things that they regret, things that often cause their parents a certain amount of pain and distress. However, most children are able to put those events behind them rather quickly, moving on to better times. Unfortunately, your empathic abilities will amplify the guilt and sorrow you feel for everything that causes your parents any sort of pain. Even the slightest of things such as a little white lie can cause you to feel absolutely guilt ridden since in addition to feeling your remorse you can also feel the pain your parents experience when you lie to them. This is highly unfair, of course, but it often results in empaths developing the highest of standards in terms of morals and virtue. Developing emotional detachment, however, is highly recommended in order to lessen the effects.

Work

Another environment that can impact an empath in a really big way is the workplace. This is particularly true for any job that creates a highly competitive atmosphere. In addition to experiencing their own stress and anxiety, empaths will also experience the stress and anxiety of those around them. This can result in an empath being ten times more stressed out than anyone else at any given time. Needless to say, this needs to be avoided at all costs.

The first rule for an empath is to create boundaries within the workplace. While the knee-jerk reaction is to offer help and solace to those in need, this can prove disastrous if no limits are established. As an empath you need to ensure that you get plenty of alone time to balance your energies and recharge your batteries. The heightened emotional atmosphere within the workplace will drain you faster than any other environment, therefore you need to take extra precautions to ensure your own health and wellbeing.

Perhaps the best-case scenario is for an empath to find a job that allows them to be fairly autonomous. Although too much solitude can have its downside as well it can be a better challenge to face than that of being constantly mentally overwhelmed and emotionally exhausted. The important thing is to put your needs first at all times so as to prevent from becoming completely burned out and unable to perform your job adequately.

Extraordinary Perceptual Abilities

Fortunately, there are numerous positive ways in which your life can be significantly enhanced and enriched as a result of your inherent gift. As an empath you may find you have certain abilities that seem almost otherworldly at first. Rather than doubting or even fearing these abilities you should embrace them and develop them so that you gain every benefit that they have to offer.

One thing many empaths experience from time to time is the ability to see future or far off events. Commonly referred to as premonitions, these visions can happen quite unexpectedly, especially when the event doesn't impact the empath themselves. If you have ever seen a place or a person clearly in your mind, only to see that person or place on the news shortly afterward, you have had a premonition. This won't happen all of the time, and not all empaths have this ability. However, if you experience it you should embrace it for the miracle that it is. There probably won't be anything you can do to affect the situation, so don't feel as though you are somehow obligated to save the world. Instead, this is just a situation where your subconscious taps into the collective subconscious and discovers something interesting. The sooner you trust this ability is, the stronger it will become.

Enhanced dream states are another common phenomenon experienced by empaths. This stands to reason as dreams are born of the subconscious, just as emotions and intuition. Therefore, the stronger your skills of intuition and emotional sensing the more intense your dreams will be. At the very least you will have an increased ability to recall your dreams, something the average person usually lacks. However, the chances are your dreams will also be richer in detail, more colorful and even longer lasting as well. Even better, you may experience what are called lucid dreams in which you become aware of the fact that you are dreaming. This opens up a whole new dimension that allows you to experience anything in the dream world with the same intensity as though it were occurring in the real world.

Finally, there are those empaths who have the ability to sense beyond human or personal experience. If you have ever 'read' the mind of an animal, or sensed the needs of a plant you are one of these people. The simple truth is that thoughts and emotions are pure energy by nature, therefore empaths can perceive them regardless of their origin. After all, a thought is a thought, regardless of whether it comes from a person or a tree. Therefore, it should be just as possible to read the one as it is the other. Many empaths don't possess this skill, however, that doesn't mean that their abilities are weaker or less developed. Rather, it's a matter of frequency. While some empaths are wholly tuned in to the human frequency, others are more in tune with the frequencies of nature. If you feel more at home with nature, and you can sense the needs of plants and animals, then this is how your empathic abilities affect your life.

In the end, each person's empathic abilities will affect their lives in different and unique ways. This is because each person's abilities are different, as are the lives they lead. Therefore, what is true for one person isn't necessarily true for another. As a result, the most important thing you can do is to discover what is true for you and the methods that work best for you in terms of honing and harnessing your skills. The more in control of your skills you are the more in control of your life you will become. After all, being an empath doesn't have to be confusing and challenging, instead it can be something truly wonderful and fulfilling.

Types of Empath

You could identify with just one of these types or you could identify with all six. The types of Empath are how you relate to your gift and how it manifests most strongly for you. For some, the energy comes through emotions and feelings while for others, it emerges as having a strong sensitivity to plants and animals instead of people.

Usually, if you are a gifted Empath in one way, then you will show gifts in another. What kind of an Empath are you?

Emotional Empath

An emotional Empath is just what it sounds like: someone who strongly senses and feels the emotions of another. This is not an easy thing to have present in your life, especially if you don't know that you are an Empath and you are dealing with a lot of other people's baggage and not just your own.

This is a highly common form of empathy and will actually usually be linked to several other types. It comes with the need to have a lot of alone time and opportunities to recharge your batteries after the exhaustion of feeling so many different people's emotional energy.

You can determine if you are emotional Empath if you are always giving a lot of your time to other people and working really hard to solve their emotional problems to the point of exhaustion. People will often naturally and unconsciously cling to an emotional Empath because of how good they are at listening and how often they help make people feel better.

An emotional Empath is actually absorbing the negative feelings of another like a sponge, lifting the worries, fears, doubts of the friend in need, but then taking that energy away with them, like a garbage collector.

Emotional Empaths need a lot of focused energy clearing, grounding, and personal honesty with their own feelings and emotions to live in a healthy balance with their gifts. True emotional Empaths will also want to look for friends and partnerships that allow them to have a more balanced emotional life. Often times, emotional Empaths get involved in very toxic relationships because they are always acting as a caregiver to their partner's emotional needs and are rarely or infrequently given the same in return leading to very low energy and several negative and unhealthy side-effects.

Physical Empath

Physical Empaths are usually those who are emotional Empaths who also have the ability to perceive physical pain coming from another person. This is often a way for you to assess how someone is feeling on the physical level and is not as common as emotional empathy. If you are a physical Empath, you would know it. You would be feeling someone's pain that you were sitting next to, or take home someone's raging headache.

Have you ever heard the term "sympathy pain"? It is a real thing that can occur for any person and will often result in taking on someone's physical feelings in an empathic way. Some men have claimed to feel the labor pains of childbirth while their partners are actually giving birth to their babies. This is an example of what physical empathy might look like. For the physical Empath, however, the experiences are much more frequent and involve even the most subtle vibration of physical discomfort. It can also relate to feelings of pleasure and joy, including sexual feelings, or orgasmic moments that are felt or shared in partnership.

There are a variety of ways this "feeling" will manifest for the physical Empath and it is important to make sure that whatever you are feeling belongs to you and not to someone else, quite similar to emotional Empaths requiring boundaries with people's emotional feelings. Some hypochondriacs might just be physical/emotional Empaths who haven't identified their gifts yet.

Plant Empath

People who are plant Empaths are those who are deeply connected to the energy of living things that are not human. A plant Empath can often "hear" what a plant or living organism might need even to the point of understanding the language that they speak. Language is a strong term to describe energy. Plant Empaths are excellent at perceiving the energy of plants and what they are here for.

A green thumb is certainly a component of being empathic with plants and many people who are naturally gifted gardeners will possess varying levels and degrees of plant empathy. The best way to understand plant Empathy is to consider how you feel when you are around them. Many plants are very high in vibration, meaning they have very light and pure energy. Being around them makes most people feel good and for someone with strong plant Empath skills, it will be a much stronger sensation of joy and happiness.

To become a plant Empath all you need is to study how they want to be communicated with. Many people will read endless books about the proper way to garden or remove pests and bugs from the leaves and soil, but these are all very human concepts. What about asking the plant what it "thinks"? For the plant Empath, this wouldn't be strange at all and if you consider that they are living beings also you wouldn't hesitate to inquire what their needs are on a daily basis, just as you would a person or even an animal, which brings us to the next type of Empath...

Animal Empath

As you may have guessed from the name, an animal Empath has an ability to sense the feelings of animals. This doesn't just mean pets or domesticated animals; it can also mean a flock, a herd, or a colony. Being an animal Empath will often coincide with being an emotional Empath and sensing the feelings of people also, but for those who are especially sensitive to human emotions, the feelings of cats and dogs can be a little bit easier to manage on a day to day level.

Some animal Empaths spend their careers working with a variety of pets or species of an animal through veterinary and rescue services, while others will just live with a lot of pets and rescue animals at their homes, living in harmony with all of the animals they meet.

You don't have to be an animal Empath to appreciate animals, of course, but it is an animal Empath who can perceive the needs, feelings, and pain of an animal which comes in handy considering that animals cannot speak English to describe what they are going through. Animal Empaths pick up on those needs and can help animals through a higher sensitivity to "reading" the energy of the animal in question.

Animal Empaths are a lot like people Empaths in the way they read the energy of another and it can be through this gift that you are able to find your most fulfilling career and living situation in close company with a variety of special animal friends.

Environmental Empath

Environmental empathy has a much larger scale. For those who are environmental Empaths, they will sense the "feelings" of an entire landscape. Imagine a mountainside completely shorn of all of its trees destined for a lumber yard. Think of all of the inhabitants of the forest that were uprooted and killed so the trees could be cut.

This is what an environmental Empaths will sense: the pain of the land that has experienced destruction. They can also feel the peacefulness and harmony of the land as well and some Empaths will choose their home based on the way the landscape and environment feel.

Environmental Empaths are also capable of sensing places, not just natural landscapes. They might walk into an old building that has seen a long and violent history, noticing the energy of how hundreds of years of religious torment left many vibrations and feelings behind in the walls and floors.

When an environmental Empath walks into a building that was built on the protected and sacred land of an indigenous people without permission, they can feel the strong energy of deceit, deception, and wrongdoing. They can also feel the vibration and frequency of goodness, compassion, and sympathy in the walls of a particular structure, that could come from the way that it was built, or the business that exists inside of it.

Environmental Empaths are often activists for the Earth and her resplendent beauty, as well as for peoples and places that need a voice to celebrate them or help them avoid destruction and disharmony. It is often the case of the environmental Empath to help protect the natural world and create consciousness around the way we live on Earth.

Intuitive Empath

Intuitive Empaths are a lot like a psychic. In a way, they are psychic and are able to have a very strong sense of things to come. They are also gifted emotional Empaths and may even have all of the other empathic gifts listed above but the main gift is an ability to have clairvoyance, and psychic perception.

This will open up for those that are given permission by their early life programming, or by a personal spiritual journey that awakens the ability to see the world in this way. When we are younger, we may or may not be told that it is possible to see the world in this way and so if you are not given an attitude at an early age that you are able to be psychic, then you are not likely to grow up with that knowledge.

Many people find their psychic awareness later on in life through their own personal choices and ability to grow in that direction. Intuitive Empaths will even begin their journeys as emotional Empaths and their intuitive abilities broaden and widen over time and with experience.

Intuitive Empaths are good at predicting a moment or situation before it has happened and are also able to assess or pinpoint deeper meanings behind the emotional pain of another. Intuitive Empaths are often able to see the past lives of another person and will even have prophetic dreams and visions that shed light on important matters in their own lives and those of other people.

A psychic will not always describe themselves as an intuitive Empath, but that is essentially what they are. They can read beyond the layer of emotion and see the energy of all possibilities for someone or something in the world. It takes a lot of practice and personal growth to achieve this type of empathy, and it is possible for everyone to do it if they are inclined to walk that path.

All of these types of empathy illustrate the reality of what being a true Empath means. Feeling empathic towards someone you know, or a situation you are in is one thing; sensing, feeling, perceiving, and absorbing those feelings is quite another. Consider what type or types of Empath you are and begin to see the correlation to your life experiences as they are right now.

Finding your type is what will help you identify the best ways to take control of your gift. You may be wondering to yourself right if it is even a good thing to be an Empath. Wouldn't life be better if it wasn't so complicated and sensitive?

Pros And Cons Of Being An Empath

Depending how long you've known that you are an empath, you may be quite familiar with the pros and cons of being one. We've already covered that one of the downfalls can be the way it is a heavy burden to bear due to the outside energies and emotions you are surrounded by. However, most things in life come with both negatives and positives. The experience of feeling those emotions around you can be wonderful and helpful in many different ways.

The pros and cons can't really be separated as they are often intertwined with one another.

Empaths are listeners. They can be all sorts of joy, being outgoing and enthusiastic and generally bubbly. Their journey can be one of emotional bliss, but it can also be one of emotional turmoil since empaths can be weighed down with mood swings galore. This is because their moods are not always their own. If empaths don't fully understand and differentiate their own thoughts and feelings from those of others, they can have fluctuating mood swings that literally change with the speed of flicking a switch on and off.

As with the good, being an empath can come with feelings of depression, anxiety, panic, fear, and sorrow. Without having any control over these feelings, you can be experiencing the suffering of others. It's a very difficult thing to have to handle and shouldn't be done so alone.

This is where compassion comes in. An empath should have at least one person they can turn to in the throes of these mood swings because being left alone can be detrimental to mental and physical health. Find someone, be it a friend or a partner or a family member, who you can turn to when things get too overwhelming for you. Whoever you find, make sure to tell them that all you really need from them is empathic love—the ability to show compassion without judging you. This may help you in recovery from these overwhelming moments.

Most empaths, unless they have gone on their own journeys of self-discovery and self-acceptance, don't actually know or understand what's going on within. They don't know that they're feeling another person's emotions like they are their own emotions. This can quite obviously lead to a myriad of feelings such as confusion, particularly if things were grand in one moment and terrible in the next. Understanding their empathic connection is a part of the journey.

It's easier for an empath to withhold their feelings and emotions than it is for others. They want to do their best not to be barraged by the feelings and emotions of others. In doing so, they often become reclusive and learn to block out these feelings. The downside of this is that they can end up bottling up their own emotions or building walls so high that they don't ever let anyone else in. This can definitely be bad for an empath—or anyone for that matter—because the longer you allow these feelings and emotions to build up inside yourself, the more power they build up. Eventually, they can explode and leave behind a lot of damage to both the empath and those around the empath. This can create an unstable environment, a mental/emotional breakdown, and/or an actual disease. Expressing yourself honestly is a choice, but it is a great form of healing.

Cons of Being an Empath

Some of these can count as pros depending on how you look at them. You'll notice how short this list is compared to the list of pros. This is because being an empath is truly a positive blessing if you understand your gift properly.

- You are easily overwhelmed. Wherever there are lots of people, you can be overwhelmed with the feelings and emotions emanating off of those that surround you. Sometimes you can be in a room with one person and still feel this way. This is why it is so important not to bottle things up.

- Addictive personalities. Empaths are prone to looking for ways to escape or block out the emotions of others. This means that they sometimes turn toward addictive substances such as sex, drugs, and alcohol. Learning to protect yourself and your energy means that you won't be struck with the need to escape these things. Instead, you will know how to cope with them properly.

- Media can be devastating. Some empaths turn away from media altogether. They can feel the emotions of others so strongly that even reading a newspaper is too much for them. It is a harsh world out there.

- Empaths can pick up both mental and physical ailments that others may suffer from. This can happen even if you don't come into contact with the other person, depending on how strong your gift is. Needless to say, no one wants to suffer this way.

- Intuition can be hurtful when you know that someone you care about is lying to you or keeping secrets from you. The ability to know and feel these things can be difficult, particularly if you can't prove such things. Try to surround yourself with people who are like minded to prevent feeling this way on a regular basis.

- We don't really have a home. Empaths are natural wanderers. After a certain amount of time, we can often feel foreign in places we once cherished. Our intuition implores with us to explore the great big world. Due to this, we're rarely ever satisfied with one place, but it does mean we make brilliant travelers.

Pros of Being an Empath

Well, we covered the cons, which I admit were pretty bad. Now we get to look at the reasons why being an empath truly is a gift. Bear with me here, because it's a pretty long list of reasons.

- Empaths are natural healers in many different forms: emotional, physical, environmental, animal, you name it. They can use their touch, their voice, and their creativity to do so. Most empaths end up on a path of healing because they simply have that pull toward their profession.

- As tough as crowds may be for an empath, the small circle they often end up building for themselves is a strong one. Once an empath makes a connection with someone, they are incredibly loyal and loving. We hold onto our loved ones tightly because we don't want to let the good ones go.

- Okay, we already know this one, but empaths love an insane amount. Their hearts are just bigger than most. Being so overloaded with all these feelings makes faking them difficult.

- That gut instinct is extremely strong and if you listen to it, I'm pretty sure you could conquer the world if you wanted to. Listen to that sixth sense of yours because it could save you from potential dangers if it hasn't already.

- Along with having an extremely strong sense of intuition, we also have amazing senses. It isn't only emotions and feelings that are heightened. If you find yourself enjoying a myriad of sensations with a lot more intensity than those around you, you can chalk that up to being an empath. We have heightened senses that allow us to better enjoy our food, beverages, flowers, essential oils, touch, and so forth. Admittedly, these can sometimes overwhelm us, but they could also help save lives. How, you might ask? Well, if you work on increasing a certain sense, such as smell, you could be able to track down death or disease in animals, people, and/or nature.

- I know we said that the weight of other people's emotions is a burden and we're really prone to lows, but we've also got the other end of the spectrum. We have great highs, too. Most empaths actually have a deep enthusiasm for life, and when we are enjoying it, we experience joy intensely.

- Empaths have an abundance of creativity! We think and see things differently. Our art is not the only creative aspect of our life, but so are our experiences, situations, and prospects. Now, you've probably had the misfortune of being told that the way you think about and/or do things is wrong, but it's a capacity all your own. Don't let anyone take that unusual creativity away from you, and let it shine brightly instead.

- This Is yet another con that also turns out to be a pro, but we can't be lied to. We are good at reading people's thoughts, feelings, and emotions. This means that we can tell when people are lying, we can tell when people aren't okay, and we can tell when people are bad news.

- Empaths can read emotional and nonverbal cues really well. It's a talent in numerous places. Due to our good senses, we can even sense the needs of those who do not speak, such as animals and plants, but also the body and babies.

- An empath generally has a craving to make the world a better place. This isn't a desire that you should ever feel ashamed of. We are capable of bringing plenty of positive changes to this world, and when we can, we should. There are already too many people turning blind eyes. Let's work on correcting the wrongs happening around us—together.

- It's especially important for us to change the world considering our pull to it. We are children of nature. It's one of the best ways to de-stress, and it can provide peace and comfort.

- To some, this might seem more like a con, but find that it's pretty cool to be able to recharge on our own. We require a certain level of alone time to recuperate. It is because of this that we are self-aware, and think it's great to be self-aware.

How Empaths Can Understand and Help Other People

We've already established that they're drawn to healing and bear the type of personality that wants the world to be a better place, but how do they go about making it one? Sure, compassion is a huge part of empathy, but what else can they do? I'd be happy to tell you.

The good that an empath wishes to do—or, rather, is capable of doing—is quite dependent on what type of empath they are. Naturally, pardon the pun, the environmental/geomantic empath has more of a pull to fix the earth. This is the same for the plant/flora empath. When an empath homes their gifts, they can use them to maintain balance and restore harmony into the world. They have their own unique ways of doing this. Empaths are fantastic listeners. They genuinely care about and enjoy learning about others, mostly because they can feel the emotions of the other person. There's a sort of rush you feel when someone tells you their stories as it can feel as though you were actually there. When someone needs support, an empath can perceive that and provide it accordingly. The empath can sense things like fear or danger, and if they've strengthened their gifts or are attuned to them, they can use the skills and adaptations they've developed to remove themselves and others from such a situation. They don't talk about themselves much, but if they do, it reveals that they have a great deal of trust in the person they're sharing with. Often, however, people seem to trust them quickly. This is because they relate to others in their own unique way.

It is because of this relatability that people feel a pull toward empaths. It doesn't matter if the empath is aware of their empathic abilities; people will still be drawn to them. People are willing to pour their hearts and souls out to empaths who are complete strangers without necessarily intending to do so. It happens on a subconscious level.

Needless to say, sometimes the empath needs that release too. That's why it's imperative that they find some of their own kind or they keep those special friends close. They're exceptional people.

Another way empath uses their abilities to bring good into the world is the ability to solve problems. Since they enjoy learning as much as they do, they study many things, and this means they are constantly sharpening their minds. Sometimes this is a subconscious action. The empath brings new meaning to the saying: "Where there is a will, there is a way."

Though it helps others, you should be wary of the fact that people will often want to offload their problems onto you. These people might not even know you. If you don't keep your guard up and strengthen your energy, these problems can convert into being your problems. Make sure that you keep the two separates. You don't want to be dragged on. Be honest with yourself and others. If a situation feels like it is going to bring negativity your way, it is okay to take a step back and tell the other person that you can't handle it. This is an act of self-preservation.

I know that sometimes it might feel like you are thrown into scenarios aimlessly and in them, you drink up the emotions of others, but you are stronger than you think. Empaths have to be strong to be able to carry both their own feelings and the feelings of others. Consider yourself a type of energy warrior. You absorb all this energy and transform it into something valuable. You have the ability to shift the negative to positive. Purify the world. If anyone can do it, an empath can.

Some empaths find that they need to be in a constant state of compassion in order not to suffer adverse effects from outside influences. Others try to be as open as they can be, allowing each feeling and sensation to pass through without much notice, and in doing so, they release all judgment and try to be as honest and carefree as possible. Then there are the empaths who believe in crystal healing in order to transfer and create energetic healing. The empath who heals the world in whatever manner they need to is the empath who has a great sense of inner peace and balance because they know that they are following their calling in life.

If you've already found what you're meant to be doing—say, for instance, mine is releasing my creativity into the world in any manner I deem appropriate—then you know what I mean by feeling a sense of balance. If you're still looking, don't give up. Follow your intuition and it won't lead you astray. Bear in mind that you may fail a few times. You may think that you've found that thing you're meant to be doing only to realize that it was nothing more than a step toward where you're meant to be. Keep searching even when you hit this wall. You are on the journey you are following for a reason. That reason will reveal itself to you soon. An empath's gut is usually right.

Importance Of Empathy

Why Is It Important To Apply Empathy In Real Life?

Without empathy, people would go about their lives without considering the feelings and thoughts of other people. Every person has differing perspectives on life; therefore, if we did not have something that made us accommodate each other, life would be very complicated. We all experience moods, joy, sadness, pain hurt et cetera, and if we focus only on the things happening in our lives, we will limit our capabilities. It is easy to jump into conclusions if we do not take a moment to truly understand what the other people stand for. Lack of empathy normally leads to bad feelings, misunderstandings, poor morale, conflict, and even divorce.

When one uses empathy in real life to understand why a person is angry, or a child is throwing a tantrum, he/she might learn about things in their lives that trigger the behavior. For example, one might find that something happened at home, thus pushing the angry person to act out or that the child did not have a meal in the morning thus they are not okay.

Empathy enables one to ask questions about the situation or behavior of another person before taking a defensive stance or reacting to some emotions. There may still be the need for disciplinary action, but one should use empathy first. Empathy makes a person feel valued and understood even if they are punished for the wrong deeds, and as such, they will accept responsibility for their action. Empathy is currently the missing link in schools, families, workplaces, and the world at large.

There are a few misunderstandings that arise when one is applying empathy in real life. Some people believe that being empathetic involves agreeing with the opinion of everybody else. That is wrong and will only lead to exhaustion. Understand the perceptions of the other person, acknowledge them but you do not have to sing along every tune.

Other people believe that being empathetic involves doing what everyone else wants or doing anything to make others happy. That is wrong. You are not obligated to please everyone; you do not have to cooperate in every other situation. Just because you fail to accommodate every other matter does not mean that you are evil. The world is complicated; therefore, use empathy but do not agree with everything.

Empathy does not mean being there for someone for a lifetime. After listening to a person and offering a solution, you do not have to always be there for them, you have other tasks to accomplish and if you feel that the person is just using you, walk away. Empathy does not mean you should have no ego or intention. Once you assist someone, allow your ego to help you walk away or change the discussion.

Applying empathy in real life can be challenging therefore, there are investments that one needs to make and they include time, patience and proactivity.

1. Time

It takes some time for one to listen to others, pay attention and not jump into conclusions. Coming up with good solutions also takes time. In most cases, we want to arrive at an answer very first without taking the time to understand; this only leads to more problems. Empathy is like watching sand draining in an hourglass; it takes time, but not that much time, and it is very satisfying.

2. Patience

Empathy does not only take time; it requires a lot of patience. Paying attention to someone, listening to everything they are saying, and selecting a comprehensive solution takes a lot more than just jumping into conclusions, listing arguments and repeating an opinion. Normally people fail to give the patience and attention required when making conversations; therefore, it becomes harder than it should be.

3. It takes proactivity

Some people think that empathy should only be given when both parties have something to gain. In the real sense, we should show empathy even to people who show no sign of understanding our perspectives and opinions. This can be very frustrating, and one might find it very unfair, but empathy begins with you. It will not work if both of you wait on each other to start the conversation.

4. Be the role model, set the example, be a good listener and do not talk until the other person is done. Understand the opinions of other people but remember you do not have to agree with them. Being empathetic can be a tough challenge but still, there are many people that practice it. Apply empathy every day and enjoy the benefits.

Empathic Listening Techniques

How to Listen With Your Heart

Of all of the talents an Empath possesses, listening may be one of the most notable. Listening skills are effective in any situation and are what help us to engage more fully with the world around us. When you can hear what is going on, you can participate more closely and provide a keener sense of understanding. You can also hear things on another level—things that are unspoken but nevertheless still communicating to us through body language, gestures, facial expressions, and energy.

For the Empath, listening comes naturally and so does absorbing energy from the person you are talking to. This can mean that you end up taking on a lot of negativity, anger, frustration, and other uncomfortable emotions. As you start to feel the effects of these feelings, it can make it harder to listen well and comfortably. The ability to listen can get upset by the emotional energy of the people around you and can distort your emotional state as well.

Finding your tactics for listening from the heart can be helpful, and with a little practice, you can learn how to compliment being a heartfelt listener while still protecting and shielding your energy from being disrupted from the negativity involved. As an Empath myself, I have tried a variety of techniques and models to help me find the best approach to being a better empathic listener without feeling drained by other people's emotions.

You can use one or all of these methods to help you better explore the best ways to provide you with grounding and centeredness while taking in, and not taking on, the feelings of the people in your life. As you read, try to keep in mind that some of these techniques will work better in some situations than in others. Use your intuition and your best judgment to decide.

Eye Contact And Lip Reading

You would be surprised at how many people talk to each other and don't make eye contact. Often when someone is telling a story, they will look in a variety of directions, looking for their thoughts, their memories, the information they want to tell you, and so on. They might also be avoiding eye contact because of insecurity or they are avoiding details to their story, intentionally leaving out things they don't want you to know.

You can tell a lot about a person based on the amount of eye contact they are willing to make. Empaths may feel a need to protect themselves by making less eye contact and just listening to words. The eyes are the window to the soul and if you are already feeling intense emotions radiating off of the person you are speaking to, then you are probably wanting to keep your distance by limiting how deeply you are peering into their soul.

The amazing thing is that focusing on someone's eyes can actually help you stay grounded and centered so that you can be a better listener. When you are only focusing on one point on someone's face, you are that much more capable of hearing all of the words they are speaking to you. You can perceive more of their tender feelings and perhaps see more deeply beyond the surface of what they are communicating. The eyes speak volumes and carry a lot of information without the use of words.

If you are practicing listening from the heart, look into the eyes of another because this is where your heart can connect to theirs. The eyes will show you what they are communicating non-verbally so that you can listen on a deeper level. Words are words, and they will explain a lot, but they might not explain everything. The eyes register so many different thoughts and feelings; they have their own "body language".

With the eyes are representing the deeper emotional layers, the lips are making the words form and have a voice. You can better and more clearly hear what someone is saying if you can see what they want you to hear. Lip reading is a skill that comes with a good deal of practice. Many deaf people use lip reading to "hear" people when they are talking. You can also use lip reading if you are not deaf to improve your listening skills.

You may be thinking, how can watching someone's mouth make me a better, more heartfelt listener? The answer is that when you are giving your time and energy to focusing on everything someone is saying, then you can truly hear their voice, their feelings, their emotions, without congesting the experience with outside influences, other people, your own thoughts and feelings, and more.

Lip reading grants you an opportunity to harness your focus and intentions. You are there to listen and as an Empath, you may be more naturally drawn to the other elements of the conversation, like how the person is feeling energetically, or whether or not the waiter remembered your order because he seemed so tense, or if your car was parked in no parking zone, because you forgot to check.

Distractions make it harder to listen well and so when you are focusing on meeting the eyes and reading the lips, then you are truly listening. Heartfelt listening naturally occurs when you are able to focus and especially if you are an empathic person when you use this technique.

The next question that usually comes up is, how can I make eye contact and lip-read at the same time? It's actually quite simple and comes with practice as well. Fortunately, the eyes and the mouth are not too far apart from each other and so you can take in most of the face all at once. While you are maintaining eye contact you can use peripheral vision to absorb the movement of the lips as they are talking. You may notice that it isn't difficult at all, to see both at once. Practice with a partner, friend, or loved one, or even try it by watching yourself talk in the mirror.

The opening of the heart to another comes through the windows to the soul and the voice of their truth. You can use this technique to help you gain clear focus and attention as you are listening from the heart and keeping yourself connected without absorbing unwanted emotional energy. Having something to focus on can actually help keep you grounded, so remember to listen with your eyes.

Hearing Their Wants Vs. Needs

While you are practicing listening with your eyes, you can also practice looking for keywords that help you understand the person on a deeper level. Many of us will start to describe a situation and within our story describe certain feelings or conditions of the situation. As we do so we start to paint a picture of what it is we want vs. what it is we need.

So, what's the difference anyway? A want is something that is desired, hoped for, longed for, sometimes repressed and never spoken of. A want is that which tells the truth of what we are feeling about how our lives should look to us and not how they are represented under the current conditions. A need is what has to happen in order for you to feel safe, secure, relaxed, alive, surviving and thriving. Everyone has basic needs and when those needs are not being met, it can be hard for us to have the wants we desire. The problem is in the question: what do they want vs. what do they need?

Being able to discern these two variables helps you become not only a better listener but more capable of helping someone resolve their issues without getting too involved. Empaths tend to want to just feel the feelings because they are naturally inclined to do so and when you are only just relating to the emotions and not offering a good listening ear with possible solutions, both of you will wallow in emotions for the rest of the conversation.

The Listening Bubble

It sounds like a magical place or the title of a fantasy novel, and you could see it that way after I describe to you what the Listening Bubble is. Creative visualization is a very useful tool for a variety of reasons. It can help you find yourself in a meditative state more easily and has even been proven to help people heal physical wounds in their bodies, simply by picturing it healing and dissolving.

The Listening Bubble is a creative visualization technique that will make sure you are able to completely focus on the person who you are talking to. There are so many things that can distract us from being a good listener and when we are able to be in a position of focus, we hear what we need to hear and we can interpret the signals and messages coming to us energetically from the other person.

The general idea of the Listening Bubble is that you are encapsulating yourselves in a space that will keep you connected to each other and focused on the conversation. The person you are talking to won't see it because it will be projected from your consciousness and is imagery from your mind. Essentially, you project the idea of a bubble around you that keeps out other energies and closes you off to one another.

CPSIA information can be obtained
at www.ICGtesting.com
Printed in the USA
BVHW090949030621
608731BV00010B/1661

9 781802 102345